OUTDOOR SURVIVAL SKILLS

Special Note from the Author

In 35 years of living in the mountains and deserts of the West, I have had many opportunities to teach and organize courses for individuals and groups. There are always seekers camping at the door of my lodge, wanting to learn from the source. In recent times the numbers of campers have increased. I have learned to welcome them in a more productive way, by calling upon others who have skills and the deeper desert feelings required for living off the land. Together we have scouted many trails for sincere students who want to learn by doing. There has never been such a unique group of the old masters to sit at the feet of. For more information write to:

Anasazi
P.O. Box 795
Payson, Arizona 85547

Sincerely,

Larry D. Olsen

OUTDOOR SURVIVAL SKILLS

Larry Dean Olsen

Chicago Review Press
Chicago, Illinois

©1990 by Larry Dean Olsen. All rights reserved
Published 1967, 1969, 1970, 1973, by Brigham Young
University Press, Provo, Utah.
Fifth edition 1990
Published by Chicago Review Press, Chicago
Printed in the United States of America

10 9 8 7 6 5 4 3 2

ISBN 1-55652-084-0

Library of Congress Cataloging-in-Publication Data

Olsen, Larry Dean, 1939–
    Outdoor survival skills / Larry Dean Olsen. — 5th ed.
      p.   cm.
   ISBN 1-55652-084-0 : $11.95
   1. Wilderness survival.   I. Title.
  GV200.5.047   1990
  613.6′9—dc20   89–49670
                                   CIP

To my father

CONTENTS

christmas
1992

glad you enjoy
outdoors as
much as I do.

Love -:-
Laurie

FOREWORD

A sad notion prevails in many circles today that the answer to our future is in our past. Certainly we have made a mess of things in terms of the environment we are to live in. Just where we are going in this direction is a question we should all ask ourselves. Where, after all, has modern technology led us regarding the air we breathe, the food we eat, and the land we live on?

This question is of major importance in *Jeremiah Johnson,* a film that director Sydney Pollack and I made for Warner Bros. The disregard for the environment today is pronounced by the high regard the early trappers had for the land yesterday. In order to properly document a single man's struggles for survival in the wilderness we wanted to have a technical adviser—someone who could give us detailed facts about how a man really did build a fire, set a trap, build shelter, shore up against the elements.

Since my home is in the mountains in Utah, I have become acquainted with the survival programs of Larry Dean Olsen at Brigham Young University in Provo and I believe his book *Outdoor Survival Skills* to be the finest of its kind. I contacted Mr. Olsen and asked if he would serve as our technical consultant. He gladly obliged and his efforts have given us a truthful and interesting documentation of an early life-style in America. His knowledge of man's conditioning to snow and the high country as well as to heat and the barren desert country is enormous. As an actor, I am very concerned about detail and authenticity, and I am comfortable that the accounts of an early life-style in this film are accurate. Mr. Olsen's tireless efforts and superior ability have made this possible.

Robert Redford
Warner Bros. Studios
Burbank, California

Editorial Comment

In an age characterized by leisure, most people depend too much on push buttons, time clocks, and other indoor conveniences for their daily survival. Consequently, they do not develop the abilities or skills which could enable them to survive stresses encountered in the wilds. History is full of war-ruined civilizations that have fallen from indoor luxury to outdoor desperation in only a few hours.

For the Stone Age man, necessity was the mother of invention, and he adapted to her toughest demands. Today, however, the mother of invention is probably leisure—or it can be if man deliberately uses that leisure to seek challenge. If he desires to combine the toughest of his ancestors with his own intellectual prowess in order to become a fully developed man prepared for the worst of the best, he is wise; he learns from yesterday. Outdoor Survival Skills *allows today's reader to bridge the gap.*

The author, Larry Dean Olsen, was born in 1939, near Jerome, Idaho. He grew up interested in the great desert wastelands of the western United States and the ancient Indian inhabitants of these deserts. As a boy, Larry trekked into remote canyon areas and became adept at living off the land.

Larry's mentors include:

1. Richard Olsen (Coyote Man), veteran trapper who lives in the vast Shoshone Deserts of Idaho and makes his living trapping, hunting, and guiding.

2. The late Albert Taylor, Paiute Indian, desert hermit of Columbet Creek. Albert taught Larry about the animals of the desert and of the little-known legends and history of his desert canyon home.

Larry's training came as a result of the great amount of time he spent as a boy roaming in the desert. His personal relationship with the wilderness led him to test all aspects of living off the land and experiencing survival at its most primitive level. He emulated the Anasazi or Ancient Ones and carefully replicated the lifestyle of the Primitive Paiutes of the Great Basin Plateau areas of the western United States.

Using tools and weapons of stone and bone, digging roots and trapping game, suffering cold nights without bedding and hot days without water or even shoes, Larry has gained a unique concept of man in nature. He has learned from the harsh environment how to be gentle and comfortable on the land.

In the 1960's Larry began teaching classes in outdoor survival in the Division of Continuing Education at Brigham Young University in Provo, Utah, sponsored by the Department of Youth Leadership. His caveman approach to survival, based on the idea that survival training is best achieved by learning to live off the land without previously manufactured gear, has won wide approval. His lectures and wilderness laboratories, which focus primarily on survival in the western United States, have been highly valuable to participants. Even the few who have found it difficult to "eat to live" rather than to "live to eat" have gained a respect for nature and the way that man can be a part of it. Larry's mastery of primitive skills has made him confident that survival living need not be an ordeal once a person has learned to adjust to the plunge from the space age into the stone age.

Larry established primitive living courses at BYU and other places throughout the United States and Canada. More than 10,000 students have participated in his wilderness laboratories, field-testing his concepts. Enthusiastic about the results, many upon returning have commented with awe: "We hadn't food, shoes, bedding, or implements of any kind. Just the shirts on our backs—and we survived!" This national award-winning course uses the stress of actual 26-day trips into the mountains and deserts of the West as a living experience for both adults and youth. The program has opened up a new area in survival training by providing a vehicle for helping young men and women establish lasting values, exercise courage in the face of seemingly insurmountable obstacles, and above all, develop a compassionate respect for human life and its relationship to nature. Many courses continue today and are popular with all age groups.

Larry wrote the first editon of Outdoor Survival Skills for his students. The book has created an enthusiasm for outdoor education concepts. There are numerous requests for this national best-seller which has become a favorite of people all over America. Outdoor Survival Skills is also well known to the National Parks Service and is sold in England, Canada, and Italy. It is most popular among young adult groups who seek relevant experience with the land. This new, revised edition contains many more skills and concepts which further enhances the quality of primitive skills.

In the last few years Larry has developed courses for private organizations and consults with the leadership of many outdoor programs. In all this, he has retained a quiet ability to fade into the desert and solitude. This fact alone holds Larry in the ranks of the present, yet casts him in the honored position of a "legend in his own time." He is the mentor, the shadow of nearly every existent living off the land philosophy in vogue today. He is the Baden Powell of primitive outdoor education, and the living Stalking Wolf of the wilderness. He is "Shadow Man."

In 1988, after many years of desert adventures, Larry was persuaded to write his own history. The series, Shadow Man, begins publication in 1989 and is eagerly awaited by readers throughout the world. The account of this man's unique life and the events leading up to his establishment of a true primitive survival style in our times will not be lost.

ACKNOWLEDGMENTS

The very nature of presenting a publication based on personal experiences and training must involve the participants who shared those moments. My wife, Sherrel, has cooked my meals for many moons in caves and under open skies. Lonny Paul Newman has accompanied me on some of the most severe tests of living off the land. Jim L. Winder, a skilled hunter and endurer, has tested with me some of the materials discussed herein. Robert L. Burnham has been my companion in primitive living and has shared his skills with me. The late Norman Herrett of the Herrett Museum in Twin Falls, Idaho, has brought to the public a form of education that makes the primitive mind live in the minds of people today. Richard A. Olsen and the late Albert Taylor have been my mentors and teachers. Thomas A. James and Thane J. Packer first encouraged me in the idea that outdoor survival should be offered in the education of all people, and helped to see it made possible on the Brigham Young University campus. Fred Bohman has given me valuable technical assistance on plants and pictures. Dan Smith is responsible for many of the pictures. William Whitaker and Ural Latham have supplied the sketches. Evard Gibby has supplied pictures for the new edition. My children, Farah, Jane, Lori, Paul, Tonia, Yolanda, Reuben, Nathan, Enoch, Joshua, Amber, and Luke gave assistance in revision, photos and skills for this present edition. To all of these people and to the more than 10,000 students who have field-tested the concepts in this book—thanks.

OUTDOOR SURVIVAL SKILLS

1

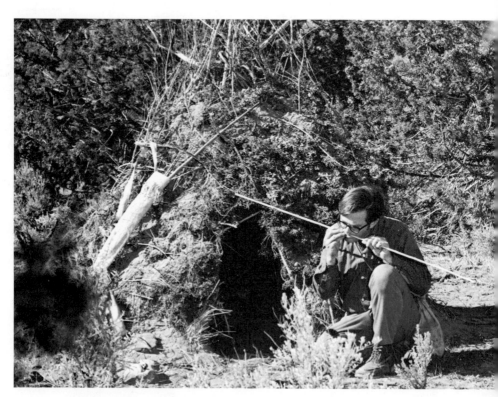

Fig. 1. The author straightening an arrow shaft

INTRODUCTION

Philosophy of a Caveman

It is contested from time to time that true survival is measured by one's capacity to stay put and prepared with a super pack of hauled-in safeguards; that learning edible plants and trapping and hunting skills are not necessary since most lost persons are rescued within 72 hours anyway. Without negating the wisdom of preparation and safeguard I would say that the philosophy behind this modern dependency is still a dangerous one. Because of confidence and practice, when one learns to live off the land entirely, being lost is no longer life threatening. Any manufactured item, such as a good knife or sleeping bag, then becomes a useful and appreciated luxury, but not a dire necessity!

Example: On a particularly dry day, Zeke Sanchez stepped from a small boat onto a bleak stretch of the shore of Lake Powell in southern Utah. The man who owned the boat and had given us the ride across the lake, stared open mouthed as Zeke handed me his gear and bid me farewell. He was on his way to catch up with a group of students and leaders about three days ahead of him in some of the most beautiful but forbidding desert land in North America. He was dressed in jeans, boots, and a long-sleeved shirt, and on his head was tied a large bandanna. That was all. The boatman called out to Zeke, "What about your pack?"

"He doesn't want it," I interrupted. "He needs to travel fast to catch the group before the week is over."

1

Fig. 2. Sharpening a stone knife

Fig. 3. Using a flint knife

Fig. 4. Starting a fire with the bow drill

"But . . . but he can't live out there without *something*!" said the boatman. "What about a canteen, sleeping bag, and something to eat?"

"He knows where the water is, he sleeps on a coal bed, and the roots are easy digging," I assured him.

Zeke disappeared over the first sand ridge of Iron Top Mesa and the boatman took me across the lake, talking all the while of unsuspecting men who had died in that very desert. He was certain Zeke was a dead man. I quietly acknowledged his concern, and agreed with him that the desert is indeed a dangerous place. I said even if a man is "prepared" with all the freeze dried, super lightweight and rip stop finery that technology offers, it's still dangerous. The desert has a way of getting "things" away from you. Still, without technological carry-ins, a man might not survive; that is, most men might not survive.

Although the boatman was wise to the harshness of the land and was a veteran of many desert travels and even rescue operations, he had little confidence in his, or anyone's, ability to make it out there without some basic camping and survival gear.

Zeke, on the other hand, was not merely oblivious to the reality of the desert. Instead, he possessed a oneness with that land and know how to use what was already there for survival. Zeke might have enjoyed a sleeping bag, but he was not bound to it, and traveling quickly was more important in his mind. Since he had poked his nose into many crevices in times past, he knew how and

Fig. 5. Using a pump drill

3

where to look for water rather than scenery, and so he was outfitted completely.

In the realm of wilderness, one must realize that there is not a single condition of extremity that is entirely without purpose. Every hour is beneficial to all those who make it their study and aim to improve upon the experience they gain. What becomes a survival situation to one person may not concern another. Besides, who can count on being rescued within 72 hours? It's just not a very personal statistic!

Three days later, Zeke caught up to his student group, well watered and sassy from eating pack rat, cicadas, mahonia berries, biscuit roots, chenopodium and cactus fruits. He sported two new ratskin possible pouches, a woven rice grass sleeping mat, a grease-wood digging stick, two dozen Paiute deadfall triggers, fire sticks, twenty feet of cliffrose rope, a jasper knife, a bone weaving awl, an unfinished serviceberry bow stave, and a whole bundle of reed grass arrow shafts.

Survival studies have shown that those who adapt successfully in a stress situation share some common attributes which set them apart from those who don't. A survivor possesses determination, a positive degree of stubbornness, well-defined values, self-direction, and a belief in the goodness of mankind. He is also cooperative. He does not feel that man's basic nature is to promote only self-interest; instead, he believes that most men are good and concerned about other people. Consequently, he is active in daily life and is usually a leader, though he may also belong to groups as a strong follower.

A survivor is also kind to himself. He does not fear pain or discomfort, nor does he seek to punish himself with them. He is not a self-hater. Even the most difficult existence is acceptable to him if it is beyond his ability to change it. Otherwise he will fight for change. He knows the odds.

Because an aura of timelessness exists in a survival situation, a person cannot allow himself to be overcome by the duration or the quality of his existence. A survivor accepts it as it is and improves it from that standpoint. One of civilized man's greatest weaknesses in a stress condition is his lack of ability to do this easily. If punching a time clock improves efficiency, it may conversely jangle a man's ability to endure to the end—that is, if he lets it.

A survivor also possesses a utopian attitude. This is not a reflection of any comfort orientation but is evidence of an artistic

4

nature. He makes even the most miserable existence seem like millennial splendor. I have witnessed this in my best students. Their digging sticks are works of art, their deadfalls ingenious, and their camps miracles of compactness and industry. There is nothing crude in the primitive existence of these people.

Stone Age living implies two things: first, an immersion within the affective domain of life and secondly, a life centered away from comfort and ease. Reasons for this may rest in meaning and time.

Affective living places some of the meanings of life in the world of work—of doing. Priorities in a hand-to-mouth existence quickly force industry to an exalted plane. If not, existence would become unbearable. Activity and industry merged with increased spiritual insight form a union that may preserve life beyond the normal limits.

Life on a higher plane than comfort and ease may seem strange in our culture, but it is an important quality of men who survive. This point has grave consequences for the comfort-oriented man lost in the wilderness. In Utah a man once died of dehydration beside a desert stream because the water was uncomfortably dirty.

Time is life, and where existence is reduced to a hand-to-mouth level, comfort must take a second seat. In survival terms we might say that comfort only gets in the way. In a literal sense a strong man may die of exposure if he neglects himself, but he may also die if he babies himself.

Lessons of survival learned in a classroom or laboratory setting may be helpful, but they will never replace direct application. My own experience has taught me that it is possible to rise above the comfort-seeking level in a primitive situation and establish priorities which not only insure my survival but grant me the added qualities of confidence and serenity as I attempt to exist in my environment. Even when the going gets rough and death becomes a grim possibility, that confidence and serenity never leave; thus struggles become challenges and my mind is better able to function without fear or panic.

I am reminded of the man who, alone in a vast desert with no hat, no water, and a broken leg, pulled himself up on one bruised and battered elbow and smiled at a bunch of dry grass, saying, "You know, if this keeps up I *might* get discouraged."

Through the years I have presented the challenge of primitive survival to several thousand students. Under some of the toughest wilderness conditions these students have tramped hundreds of miles across rivers, mountains, and deserts of the West. There is no question in my mind that young people today are as tough as their pioneer forefathers. However, the most disturbing discovery of these expeditions has been the types of stress that cause people to give up. Many students drop in their tracks, not from physical exhaustion, but from mental anguish. They are often afraid to make the effort once the challenge is realized.

Then there is the other extreme—those who at first appearance seem not to be able to make it but who plow through to the end despite their physical limitations. They have their minds set on success. Incidents from two expeditions illustrate this positive stubbornness in a survival situation.

John was overweight and a slow hiker. He found the pace exhausting and breathing difficult in the intense heat of the desert. Water was scarce and the small group of students was bent on pushing to a small seep spring some twenty miles away. Worried, I assigned two students to hang back and keep an eye on him. Two instructors, in good shape, pushed ahead, running, with instructions to bring back water for the stragglers.

At the seep spring, several hours later, I was surprised to hear that John had made it completely on his own. To top it off, he had assisted one of the students assigned to him in bringing in another student who had a sprained ankle. They came in singing.

During the weeks that followed, John became the physician of his group and spent hours helping others. He made the 300-mile trek and never required more than his share of the meager food and water.

On another expedition, we had been three weeks on the trail, our destination taking us into the wind, which was blowing in the first winter storm. The terrain was steep and broken. The advance scout returned with word of a large overhanging cliff which would shelter the whole group until the storm passed. It was located about eight miles away near the top of a high ridge, and we began heading for it just as the sun went down.

We had been several days on meager rations and water, and many of the students had bad blisters which were par for any course of this kind. Our food supply consisted of a bag of flour and some Brigham brush (*Ephedra*) for making a warm drink.

The first group to reach the cave built a fire and rolled up in blankets to sleep, too worn out to eat. A short time later three more exhausted students came in with word that six others were having a rough time about three miles from the cave, halfway up the steep hill. The rest of the students were struggling up in small groups.

By this time it was dark, the wind had increased to a gale, and snow was falling. I found the group at the cave arguing with the three who had brought in the report. The three wanted the others to help make Brigham tea and ash cakes (flour and water patted into small cakes and baked in hot ashes) to take back to the struggling students below. The arguing proved futile, so the three alone prepared about fifty ash cakes and warm Brigham drink. Then one stayed at the fire cooking more food while the other two went back down the mountain with food and drink to aid the six laggers.

By two o'clock a.m. they had brought in the last of the men, fed them again, and stacked up a huge pile of firewood. They warmed cold feet, doctored blisters, and cheered hearts as best they could under the circumstances. Zeke Sanchez was one of those men, and he became a leader of many desert treks.

2

Fig. 6. Brush and bark wickiup

SHELTER

One of the first skills a person must learn is how to construct a shelter. He must also know what type of shelter is most appropriate for a given situation and that the techniques used for building it depend upon need and time. Most shelters should be built according to a few basic specifications; however, special circumstances such as rain or snowstorms or extremely cold weather may dictate any kind of makeshift protection which can be built in a hurry. Nevertheless, after a degree of comfort has been achieved, a semipermanent shelter should be constructed to assure safety in the event conditions get worse.

Building for survival requires more than a minimum of effort and calls for sound planning. Most essential to this planning is the selection of a campsite. A good campsite provides:
- Protection from wind and storms
- Protection from flash floods, rock falls, high tides
- Freedom from poisonous plants, insect pests (ants, mosquitoes, fleas), and harmful animals
- Level ground for a bed and a fireplace
- Availability of materials for making a shelter and a bed
- An inexhaustible source of firewood
- Food sources and drinking water
- Dry ground located away from creek bottoms and green grassy areas

A good fire pit is also essential to survival. As it is used primarily for heating and cooking, it should be:

■ At least eight inches deep and lined with stones
■ Surrounded with spark protectors, which can be made from green pine boughs or upright sticks. (If the protectors are placed at least six inches high, most popping sparks will be stopped.)
■ Located in a direct line with the shelter entrance and slightly forward from the center, as this allows ample space at the back of the lodge

Also of major importance in building for survival are the dimensions and strength of the shelter. It must:

■ Allow free movement around the fire
■ Provide space for a dry woodpile just inside the opening
■ Provide plenty of storage space for food and gear
■ Allow for a fair-sized fire pit for cooking and heating and enough space from walls and ceiling to prevent flames and sparks from catching in thatch materials
■ Be strong enough to withstand high winds and heavy snowfalls (Figs. 7 and 8). (There is nothing quite like having your shelter fall in on you at 3:00 a.m.) Its construction should include:

• Strong supporting poles lashed firmly, although most other poles and thatching can be laid on without lashing
• Heavy branches stacked against the finished lodge to prevent the wind from scattering the thatching when it is composed of grass and boughs
• Plenty of matting and grass for a floor covering, which must be kept at least one foot away from the fire and stirred up each evening or, even better, removed completely from the shelter and then respread—especially important in snake country

Lean-to

Easy-to-build windbreaks serve well for summer living and give ample protection in cold weather if sturdy (Fig. 9). However, they are only temporary emergency shelters. When constructed, a lean-to should provide protection from the prevailing *night* wind, contain a large reflector so that maximum heat can be obtained from the fire, and be three-sided so that maximum protection can be obtained.

Fig. 7. Framework for large shelter

Fig. 9. Three-sided lean-to

Fig. 8. Heavy thatching for sturdy shelter

11

Fig. 10. Wickiup

Fig. 11. Large wickiup

Fig. 12. Reed grass wickiup

Brush Wickiups

A good wickiup takes only a little longer to build than a lean-to and is much more serviceable (Fig. 10). This comfortable dwelling is one of the best, as it provides protection from all sides. It consists of a tripod on which a tight circle of poles is stacked to form a large tipi or cone-shaped frame. Over this frame is placed a thatching of brush, leaves, reeds, bark, rotten wood, pine boughs, and even dirt. The entrance can be large and face the rising sun, or it can be small and provide protection from all outside breezes. One can make the floor space fourteen feet across, if he uses twenty-foot poles, and provide sleeping space for eight people (Fig. 11). These rough shelters provide shelter from wind and cold, but are not generally effective in a prolonged rainstorm. More sophisticated methods are needed for a truly waterproof shelter. A pole or grass thatched wickiup will do the job.

Pole Wickiups

In heavily timbered areas, large wickiups are possible which will house several people and their gear. Gather all the dry, dead poles and long sticks in the area. A three pole tripod is erected in the same manner as a tipi.

With the tripod in place, successive poles are laid on carefully to ensure that the spread is even and smooth. No poles should stand

Fig. 13. Pole wickiup

out from the rest. Trim poles of their branches by knocking these off with a club. As the poles are laid on, the space at the top of the tripod will fill up. Shorter poles can be placed in the remaining spaces, and the wider spots near the base can be filled in with shorter slabs of bark, split wood, sticks, and short poles. The point is to fill in all the spaces with something solid.

The next step is to apply a layer of boughs, grass, and plant stalks over the outside, stuffing materials into the cracks and spaces. Start at the base of the frame and layer the covering, overlapping each tier as you go up the sides of the frame. To reach the top half of the wickiup, construct a single rung pole ladder and rest it against the frame.

When the grass and bough covering is in place, start again at the base and cover the entire wickiup with an additional layer of mulch and dirt. This will stop even a driving rain and make the shelter cozy and durable for a long period of time. It takes a while, but it is well worth the effort. To gather the mulch, select areas under large trees where the forest floor is deeply matted with pine needles, leaves, and vegetable matter. Dig out the mulch in layers, if possible, and haul it to the wickiup site in blanket bundles. The mulch can be laid on in shingle fashion or packed thickly against the sides at the base to ensure a solid base to build on. Make sure the mulch cover is thick and well packed.

Fig. 14. Grass wickiup frame

Fig. 15. Making grass thatching

The final step is to keep the mulch from blowing away by applying a last layer of poles, branches, and sticks to the outside. Just lay them against the wickiup to hold everything in place.

The final product should be a solid structure with a small entrance facing east or southeast. A fire pit is made in the center of the inside circle, and a good layer of dry grass is spread for bedding. I have built these wickiups in many areas and they have survived several winters of heavy snow, providing shelter for animals as well as humans.

Grass Thatched Wickiup

A more permanent desert camp site deserves a unique and efficient home made of grass. It is easier to build than one would think, and when finished, will withstand wind, rain, snow and even reflect cruel desert heat. However, fire has its way with this shelter and constant care must be taken to prevent flying sparks.

To build a grass wickiup, first secure three sturdy poles in the ground with the ends almost touching at the top. This is best done by scratching a circle for the wickiup on the ground and digging the post holes at least 18 inches deep, an equal distance apart around the circle. Solidly tamp the backfill around each post with a heavy pole. This tri-pole frame provides the support for the whole structure.

Fig. 16. Rod Allred by his grass thatch wickiup

Fig. 17. Grass thatch wickiup

With a hard wooden stake, pound additional holes in the ground, every 12 to 15 inches around the perimeter of the circle. Insert long trimmed willow poles in the holes to form a full frame structure (Fig. 14).

With long willow withes, bind the entire frame together, beginning about 15 inches from the bottom with the first round. Then add successive rounds about 15 inches apart clear to the top of the frame. The withe rounds should be tied to each pole in the frame. This can be done with green strips of willow bark, cattail leaves, sagebrush, cliffrone bark strips, or any other natural cordage material (Fig. 14).

It is important to construct the frame with all parts evenly spaced so that no frame poles protrude out from the cone surface, or sag inwardly. This will not only look better, but will ensure a proper lay for the grass thatching.

The next step is to harvest great armloads of long dry grass. Cut the grass in bunches or simply pull it out in hand sized clumps. Be sure to stock each armload evenly with all the root ends together. Neatly tie each bundle to prevent the grass from tangling and mixing during transportation to the wickiup site. Sometimes you have to range out for several miles to gather enough good thatching grass. There are several tall desert varieties of thatching grass including bunch grass, crested wheat, wild rye, and even June grass. The best long grass grows on steep slopes and at the base of cliffs. It is usually found lying flat in mats, pressed down from winter snow. Try to harvest only dry grass that was growing the previous season. Older grass stalks are often brittle and rotted. Green grass works well, but must be dried before use.

The grass is then carefully separated into small bundles about 1⅓ to 1½ inches in diameter with all the root ends together. Two strands of cordage are used to tie the small grass bundles to each other in a kind of "hula" skirt (Fig. 15). The first course of cordage starts about 4 inches from the root ends, with the second course of cordage being tied on at the same time approximately 4 inches up the bundles from the first cord. Each course is tied with a simple half hitch or if desired may be held in a twined weave fashion (see weaving). The twined weave is less secure, but is easier when you are using bark cordage.

Make the skirts from two to four feet long for easy handling. Roll them up and set them aside until you have enough completed to make the first course around the base of the wickiup.

To lay on the first course, select a space for the doorway. Face the doorway to the east, southeast, or south, depending on the time of year. Summer doors face east and make shade out front during the heat of afternoon. Winter doors face south and catch the sun most of the day. Starting at the selected door pole, tie the skirts in place every 12 to 18 inches along the frame. The ties can be secured to the pole frames and also to the circular withes of the frame. Make sure the grass skirt tips are resting or pressed tightly against the ground all the way around the wickiup. Bank a little dirt against them on the outside or lay some short pieces of wood against them at ground level.

When the first tier or course of grass is secured on the frame, take slender willows and tie them on the outside all the way around the base of the skirts. Tie each withe securely through the grass thatch to the frame poles. A small sharp stick will poke the holes necessary to thread the cord through the grass.

The second course of thatch is constructed and placed on the frame in the same manner, making sure that the skirts overlap almost half the length of the first course. This is important for a tight covering to the shelter. When the skirts are tied in place, run another course of willow withes around the outside, this time making sure that it holds down both the top of the first course and the overlapping second course. This will withstand strong winds (Fig. 16–17).

Continue laying on courses of thatch until the top of the shelter is reached. The upper tiers are best worked on with a single rung ladder on the outside, and something to stand on inside the shelter.

Leave the very top of the wickiup open for a smoke hole and build a small hearth near the center of the inside circle. From the inside, fill any cracks or holes with strips of loose grass and remove any hanging strands that might catch in the fire or tickle the back of your neck.

A covering for the door can be made by making an extra skirt of grass with three or more strands of weave. It may be secured to a willow frame if desired.

Living arrangements in a grass wickiup require some necessary etiquette and a lot of caution. Keep all bedding materials securely away from the fire. This can be done with small poles or stones framing the beds. Keep the ground around the fire free of straw, twigs or any burnable materials. Never step across the fire pit. Dragging feet will pull combustible materials into the pit, which may burst into flames when you are gone. It is best never to leave a flame fire burning unattended in a shelter. From experience I can say that it is not an exciting sight to light up the sky after so many hours of hard work building a warm wickiup.

Rock Shelters

The favorite natural protection of the Indian people in the West was the rock shelter, an overhanging cliff or bank that affords protection from the elements (Fig. 18). With a minimum of effort these shallow caves can be turned into first-class living quarters.

In the winter, rock shelters facing south catch the sun's warmth most of the day. For added protection low windbreaks or reflectors can be built across the front of the cave. Poles leaned against the outside edge of the roof and thatching, as in the construction of a wickiup, constitute a cave shelter that can be completely sealed from the elements.

Fig. 18. Rock shelter (cave)

Insulated Wattlework

A little more time and patience is needed in the construction of a wattlework shelter, but the comfort it provides is worth the extra effort (Fig. 19). Each wall is made with two parallel rows of stakes driven into the ground about a foot apart, willow sticks woven along the stakes to form a fairly tight mesh, and grass and other material stuffed between the two woven walls. The result is a thick, insulated wall that will stop any cold. The roof is simply made of poles and willows with grass thatching piled on top. Heavy willow rods and brush are piled on top of the grass to keep the wind from blowing it away.

Sweat Lodge

The Navajo Indians make a small earth lodge for sweating purposes, but it also serves as a warm shelter (Figs. 20 and 21). Simply a small wickiup covered with a thick layer of dirt, it should · be built over a pit large enough to accommodate at least one person and a fire pit. The earthen covering should seal off all areas where air might enter. The entrance must be small, large enough only for a person to crawl into, and should have as tight a covering as possible.

For warming this shelter a large fire must be built outside the entrance and several rocks heated. A small pit dug inside and to the left of the entrance serves as the heating pit. A person sitting inside can reach out through the entrance with a set of wooden tongs, pick a hot rock out of the fire, and pull it in, making sure that all the sparks and coals are shaken off. A single rock in the pit will heat the shelter for several hours. When it begins to cool, it can be replaced by another rock from the hot bed of coals outside.

Snow

Snow caves are the simplest to construct, as they are merely dug into a snowbank that has a good crust, but they are not generally warm (Figs. 22 and 23). If well built, however, snow shelters can be heated adequately; but if they are to be comfortable, a lot of matting and floor covering are necessary. Lean-to shelters and wickiups covered with snow are excellent.

Fig. 19. Insulated wattlework

Fig. 20. Cross section of sweat lodge

21

Fig. 21. Finished sweat lodge

ventilation hole

snow

fire shelf

sleeping shelf

snow block

Fig. 22. Snow cave

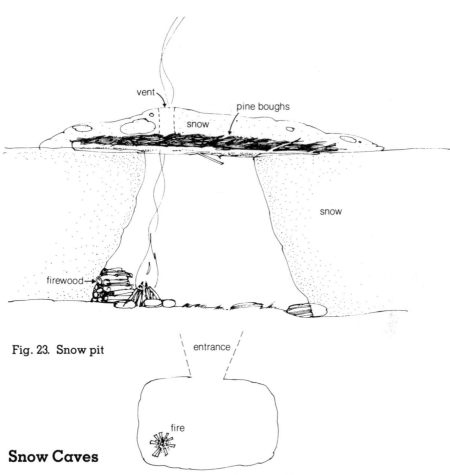

Fig. 23. Snow pit

Snow Caves

Traditional shelters of snow are at best chilly tombs to ward off more severe cold and provide protection from the wind and storm. Seldom is a snow cave suitable for comfortable housekeeping on a long-term basis unless elaborate preparations and special construction techniques are used. When the problem is survival, however, even the damp and cold of a snow cave are inviting compared to being out in the open.

In recent years many methods and styles have been tried, tested, and evaluated. Prehaps the most efficient system is one suggested by Ernest Wilkinson, a veteran wilderness guide in Colorado. With consideration for area and snow depth, I have used this method successfully:

Select a campsite away from potential avalanche or snowslide paths. Be sure there is plenty of firewood in the area. Select in this area a large deep snowdrift that has crusted over. Tramp down a good camp space in the front or lee side of the drift. Build a fire pit and a fire and pile up a snow windbreak on either side of the area. Stack up firewood for outside cooking and warmth.

Square off the front of the drift and begin digging a hall tunnel big enough to walk into, but sloped upward as you go. If possible, cut the snow out in chunks. (A good knife can be made by flattening a long stick into a blade.) Make the tunnel about 4 feet high for easy standing room and about 2¹/₂ to three feet wide. Tunnel 8 to 10 feet in if possible.

Once this initial hall tunnel is completed, construct sleeping bunks on either side of the hall. To do this, cut out the snow, beginning about 2 feet inside the hallway and continuing all the way to the back of the tunnel. Make the shelves at least 2¹/₂ feet wide and as high as possible above the sloping floor level of the hall tunnel. This way the heat will circulate high around the sleeping shelves while the cold air sinks in the hallway. The ceiling should be shaped into a dome, and the snow roof should be at least a foot thick (Fig. 22).

The entrance to the tunnel at this point is wide open, with easy access for construction, but it lets the wind blow right in. It must be sealed off. Before doing this, however, haul in all your gear and bedding materials and some small pieces of firewood. Place several inches of insulation—pine boughs, dry grass, sagebrush tops, juniper bark, and so forth—on the sleeping benches, along with whatever blankets, pads or sleeping gear you might have. Another good insulation is a row of sticks two or three inches in diameter lying side by side crosswise on the sleeping benches, covered with pine boughs. At the back of the hall tunnel, construct a separate shelf for gear storage and pad it also with branches and other insulation to keep the items from coming in direct contact with the snow.

When all the gear and bedding are in place, use the snow blocks excavated from the tunnel to rebuild the entrance. Completely seal it up and pack the cracks with snow. After it sets up for a few minutes, cut an entrance hole just large enough to crawl into. The hole should be low down near the floor of the tunnel, so that the heat, which rises, will be trapped inside the shelter around the sleeping benches. A loose piece of cloth or pile of pine boughs can be stacked in the hole after you are inside for the night, to break any wind blowing in, but the hole should not be sealed off completely.

It is not necessary to build a large fire inside for light and warmth. If a candle is available, that's all you need. Lacking candles or lamps, a fire can be built and kept very small. Make it on top of a tin can, in a tin cup, or on a small flat rock, and feed it with shavings and small twigs. In any case, create a draft for the fire by poking a small hole through the ceiling of the snow cave. Eventually the ceiling of the snow cave will glaze over from the heat and the shelter will cease to "breathe." The entrance and the smoke hole in the ceiling will help keep the air fresh and clear of smoke.

Matting and Bedding

Sleeping in some degree of comfort is also an important part of the shelter and can be achieved rather easily. Dry grass, pine boughs, sagebrush bark, cattail stalks, bulrushes, and reeds make excellent bedding, and can be found at any time of the year. In the winter, dry grass is located at the base of cliffs that face the south. Snow usually melts away in these areas and the sun keeps the grass dry. Rats nests that contain enough grass for bedding are usually found in cracks and small caves, but may contain cactus spines as well.

Hot Coal Bed

Heated ground under a bed makes even the coldest nights comfortable. But care should be taken not to allow direct contact with the hot stones. Even after several hours of cooling, the rocks will still burn holes in bedding. After the stones are heated by a fire built right in the pit, the ashes which have accumulated are scraped out before the covering of dirt is applied (Figs. 24–26).

windbreak

dry grass

bed

10 inches

dirt layer

3 inches

hot rocks

Fig. 24. Hot coal bed

Fig. 25. Hot coal bed lined with stones

Fig. 26. Removing ashes from heated bed

Fig. 27. Chimney draft bed

26

Chimney Draft Bed

The construction of this type of bed is a complicated challenge for any warm bed enthusiast, but once built, it is unequaled for comfort in cold weather (Fig. 27). Such a bed is best constructed inside a large shelter or cave since the bed itself provides very little protection from wind and storm. The more elaborate chimney draft bed illustrated here (Fig. 27) has in recent years given way to a more efficient method:

Construct a 2½-foot-diameter stone and mud oven below ground level with a 12-inch door at the very bottom of the oven. Chink the stone with a mixture of mud and grass. As the dome goes up, place the stones so that they gradually pull inward. A green willow support frame on the inside will make this part of the job easy. Just below ground level, near the top of the dome, leave a hole about 6 inches in diameter at the point where the flue trench begins, which should be downwind from the oven (Fig. 28).

Dig a trench approximately 10 inches wide and 6 inches deep in a straight line 8 feet long. Line the sides of the trench with flat stones to bring the width of the trench down to about 5 or 6 inches.

Fig. 28. Stone oven

Fig. 29. Building the trench

Fig. 30. Covering the trench

Then place wide, flat stones over the trench, completely covering it. Seal cracks and joints with the mud/grass mixture, making sure that none falls inside the trench (Fig. 29 and 30).

Place two long sticks, logs, or lines of stones parallel on either side of the flue trench and about 4 feet apart if two people are using the bed, 2¹/₂ feet if only one person is using it. Stake the logs down so they won't roll away. In the space between the logs and over the flue trench stones, fill with dry sand, dry grass and boughs to a depth of about 3 inches.

At the opposite end of the trench, construct a stone and mud chimney to a height of not less than 4 feet, the higher the better. Make sure it is airtight and sturdy with an expanding base which covers the opening to the flue trench. The flue at the top of the chimney should be about 6 inches in diameter.

Build a small fire inside the oven to dry it out and expose any leaks in the oven, along the line, or in the chimney. Fan the fire by blowing through the oven door until the smoke starts drawing through the chimney.

Fig. 31. Building the chimney

Fig. 32. Smoking chimney

Fig. 33. Completed chimney draft bed

Fig. 34. All-night comfort

Later, build a larger fire and keep it stoked until a deep bed of hot coals is formed in the oven. Fill the oven again with wood and place a slab of rock against the door, sealing out most, but not all, of the air. This will act as a damper and keep the fire burning slowly all night.

The bed will soon heat up along the flue tunnel, and two people can sleep comfortably with heat that lasts all night. A further refinement is to build an A-frame shelter over the bed which protects from the weather. A person can sleep comfortably without even a blanket in this type of arrangement.

Group Heat Trap

Occasionally a group of people may be caught in the open. Usually the best plan is to keep moving, because keeping the body in motion by hiking maintains warmth. However, in cold, windy conditions, short rest periods are essential to regain strength. Ordinarily it is advisable to stand while resting to prevent muscles from stiffening and cramping. When the distances are great, however, and longer rests are needed, it is wise to get in a restful position and develop a semi-sheltered condition to ward off the cold or wind. Failing to do this may result in a fatal loss of body heat. By forming a group heat trap or ground body shelter, people can trap a great deal of heat and maintain body temperature at a higher level while they are resting. One way to do this is as follows:

- Everyone sits shoulder-to-shoulder in a tight circle pointing the feet inward.
- Each person sits on one edge of a blanket or sleeping bag or whatever covering is available and pulls the rest of it around his back and over the top of his head.
- Hold the blanket forward with the hands or tuck it under one foot to form a sort of sitting hammock. This will relieve the strain on the back from sitting on the ground and form a canopy over the head.
- When everyone in the circle is doing this, a tight windbreak is formed with a semi-secure canopy overhead to hold in the heat. It is surprising how much warmer this arrangement is than merely wrapping up and huddling. Each person can be watched carefully for symptoms of hypothermia and the group can talk, plan, or play games to take the edge off their harsh circumstances.

3

Fig. 35. Starting a fire with the bow drill

FIRE

The importance of a good fire can hardly be underestimated. Even in warm weather a fire is essential, not only for warmth at night but for cooking, signaling, purifying water, and aiding in the manufacture of various useful items. The following methods are exhaustive and should be studied carefully. Reading about how to start a fire without matches is one thing, but doing it is another.

An inexperienced person in the wilds without matches or other modern methods of making fire will find that primitive methods are beyond his ability. On the other hand, an experienced artisan may create a good fire in less than a minute, only with materials found in nature (Fig. 35).

Success in making fires is achieved only with practice and carefully wrought equipment. No amount of effort will produce a fire when dexterity is lacking and when equipment is crude. Getting that first spark to burst into flame is somewhat of a surprise, but from that moment, it is almost certain that future attempts will be successful.

Tinder

Tinder is made from dry bark which is light and fluffy, and from shredded grass, dry moss, birds' nests, and various plant fibers.

The preparation of tinder requires special attention. It should always be finely shredded (but not powdered) so that the bundle is a soft, fluffy, fibrous mass which will not fall apart. Rubbing the bundle between the hands is perhaps the best way to make tinder light and fluffy (Fig. 36).

The following list contains the more common tinders available in nature. Others may be found by experimentation in different geographical areas.

Barks

- Cliffrose (*Cowania*): shrub—outer bark from trunk and larger limbs (Colorplate 8, p. 192)
- Cottonwood (*Populus*): tree—inner cambium layer on old dead trees (Colorplate 8, p. 192)
- Sagebrush (*Artemisia tridentata*): shrub—outer bark from trunk of larger plants (Colorplate 26, p. 210)
- Juniper (*Juniperus*): tree—outer bark from trunk of mature trees (Colorplate 15, p. 199)

Plant Fibers and Silks

- Yucca (*Yucca*): fibers from pounded dead leaves or ready-made at the base of dead plants
- Nettle (*Urtica*): fibers from pounded dead stalks (Colorplate 20, p. 204)
- Milkweed (*Asclepias*): fibers from pounded dead stalks; also silk from pods (Colorplate 16, p. 200)
- Dogbane (*Apocynum*): fibers from pounded dead stalks (Colorplate 9, p. 193)
- Thistle (*Circium*): down from tops (Colorplate 30, p. 214)
- Cattail (*typha*): down from seed heads (Colorplate 7, p. 191)
- Various grasses: dead leaf blades, partially decomposed, lying at base of plants

Flint and Steel

Steel, a luxury item, is rarely found in nature and then only if someone has left or lost it. When present in the form of a pocket-knife, nail file, and so forth, it can be used in combination with a hard stone to produce sparks hot enough to catch tinder.

Flint stones come in a wide range of types, all of which contain some silica. Agate, jasper, and quartzite are perhaps the best, though any silica stone will do. It should be broken into angular chunks to produce sharp edges. The tinder bundle must be of the finest quality material, sagebrush, cottonwood, or cliffrose bark being the best. A small nest is made in the tinder bundle and the finest shredded material is loosely sprinkled in the depression (Fig. 37).

Striking the spark takes a little practice. The best method is for a person to hold the stone in one hand and the closed blade of a pocketknife, or something similar, in the other, and with a rather loose-jointed-wrist approach, strike the sharp edge of the stone

Fig. 36. Preparing tinder

Fig. 37. Making a nest in a tinder bundle

rather severely until sparks fly off and fall onto the tinder bundle (Fig. 38). A thin wisp of smoke will signal that one has caught. Then the tinder bundle must be picked up quickly and very gently, and the spark must be blown on with short puffs of air. If the timing of these actions is just right, the spark will spread and burst into flame (Fig. 39).

A surer way of getting sparks to hold is to use specially pre-pared charred tinder. Once a fire has been produced by other means, it is a simple matter to make plenty of charred tinder for quick, easy fires later on. Manure, wood punk, or pithy plant stalks are burned until very black and then smothered in an airtight container or simply stepped on several times in very dry dust. Plant stalks should be split to expose the pith. When charred, the mate-rial can be stored in small containers or wrapped inside tinder bundles until time for use. For best results manure, punk, and pith, after charring, should be crumbled into powder.

A cotton handkerchief, a piece of cotton cloth cut from a shirt-tail, or a piece of cotton charred in the same manner is even superior to punk or pith, if it can be sacrificed. The charred mate-rial, placed in the tinder bundle, catches readily when sparks fall on it and holds longer than punk or pith. Sources of excellent charred tinder materials are:

- Masses of very soft dry rot found in rotted, fallen logs of the cottonwood tree (*Populus*) and some other trees (Colorplate 8, p. 192)
- A pithy core of superior quality found in the center stalk or spike of the yucca (*Yucca*)
- An excellent pithy core found in the stalks of the mullein (*Verbascum*) (Colorplate 19, p. 203)
- A large but rather tough pith found in the stalks of the elderberry (*Sambucus*) (Colorplates 9, p. 193)
- A soft pith found in the stalks of the sunflower (*Helianthus*) (Colorplate 30, p. 214)
- Manure: dried chunks found in ample supply in most areas frequented by game and livestock

Bow Drill

Making fire with a bow drill is a simple matter if the apparatus is constructed correctly. It has four parts: a fireboard, a drill, a socket, and a bow (Fig. 40).

Fig. 38. Striking a spark

Fig. 39. Blowing a spark into flame

Fig. 40. Bow drill

Fig. 41. Bow drill

Fig. 42. The all-important notch

Fig. 43. Getting a spark

An excellent fireboard, which should be about 1/2 inch thick, can be made from a dead cottonwood branch. A slight depression must be drilled along one edge and can be smoothed and deepened by a few turns of the bow and drill. A notch, which reaches to the center of the pith, is cut in the side of the board and catches the fine powder gound off by the drill. It is in this fine powder that the spark is formed (Figs. 41 and 42).

The drill may be of the same wood as the fireboard and should be from 8 to 12 inches long and about 3/4 of an inch in diameter. The top end is sharpened to a point while the bottom is blunt.

The socket is made by drilling a depression in any piece of hardwood or stone that fits the hand. When in use, the drill runs smoother if the socket is lubricated with grease. Enough lubrication can be obtained by rubbing the top of the drill stick through the hair or on each side of the nose. The use of water for lubricating a socket only makes it swell and bind.

The bow should be 18 to 25 inches long and about 1/2 inch in diameter. A branch with a fork on one end makes an excellent bow. The best string is a strip of 1/4-inch-wide buckskin or other leather, but substitutes can be made from plant fibers, shoelaces, or some other cord. The cord is attached to one end of the bow and twisted until it is tight and round before being tied to the other end. It is a good idea to fix one end in such a way that it may be loosened or tightened as needed. If the bow drill does not run smoothly, it may be that a little more twist in the cord is needed.

In using the bow drill, one places the fireboard on a flat piece of bark or wood. The spark will pass onto this piece and can then be carried to the tinder. Another method involves the digging of a small depression under the fireboard. The tinder is placed in the hole under the board in a position which allows the spark to fall directly into it. The proper position for working the set calls for a person to get down on one knee and place one foot on the fireboard to hold it steady. He then places the drill, with the bow cord twisted once around it, in the fireboard socket. Using the hand socket to apply pressure, he then moves the bow back and forth in a sawing motion with steady, even strokes until the drill tip is smoking well (Fig. 43). He gradually spins the drill faster and applies more pressure with the hand socket. After a lot of black dust from the drill starts collecting beside the notch and there is plenty of smoke, there should be enough heat for a spark. The drill is then carefully lifted away, and the pile of black dust is lightly fanned with the hand. If there is a spark, the pile will begin to glow. When this happens the spark must be carefully placed in the tinder and blown into flame (Figs. 44–46).

Hand Drill

The basic principle for making a fire with a hand drill is the same as that for making one with the bow drill. However, instead of using a bow and socket, the drill is simply twirled between the palms of the hands. The hands should be arched out stiffly for the best results, and the drill should be at least 16 inches long and tapered slightly from the bottom toward the top. Since this method is so difficult, it is not recommended as a sure way to get fire. Aborigines seem to have the skill necessary for this operation, and a few civilized people achieve it after much practice.

This method is speeded up when two people work together. One person spins until his hands reach the bottom of the spindle and then the other takes over at the top. In this way the spinning motion is constant (Fig. 47).

Other Methods

Various other techniques used to make fires include the fire saw, in which two sticks are rubbed together in a notch until a spark is

Fig. 44. Lifting the drill from the socket

Fig. 45. Placing the spark in tinder   Fig. 46. Blowing the spark into flame

Fig. 47. Using the hand drill

Fig. 48. Fire bundles (the top bundle has been burning 6 hours)

fire bundle

bark strips

finely shredded
bark

shredded bark

cross section showing
composition of fire bundle

cord

thinned

green wood

fire tongs

Fig. 49. Fire bundle and tongs

formed; the fire thong, in which a strong vine or rope is pulled back and forth in a split stick; and optics, in which a lens from glasses, a flashlight, field glasses, the bottom of a pop bottle, or a bottle filled with water is used to concentrate the rays of the sun.

Maintaining a Fire

Once a fire is made, a person may need to take certain precautions to keep it going. When he camps in one spot for a period of time, he can keep a fire alive through the night by building up a deep bed of hot coals and banking them with ashes and a thin layer of dirt. The important thing is to keep the wind from the coals.

Tinder can be prepared for traveling purposes from shredded bark which is baked until it is powder dry. It can then be carried in a dry container or wrapped in several strips of bark. The Paiute Indians ingeniously transported live fires over long distances by simply making a long bundle out of a core of shredded sagebrush or other bark placed on several thicknesses of dry stripped bark. Additional layers were placed on top and the whole bundle was wrapped tightly with more strips of bark. When finished, the firecarrier looked like a giant cigar about two feet long and six inches in diameter (Figs. 48 and 49). A hot coal was placed in one end and the Indian traveled with the fire carrier in his hand or stuck in his belt. Such a bundle would hold a live spark from six to twelve hours. Usually two or three bundles were made and carried. When one burned low, the Indian stopped and built a small fire, and in a few minutes he had a new supply of hot coals from which he would light another bundle.

Miscellaneous Hints

- A fire blower for stirring up dead fires can be made from any hollow stem. Canary reed grass and elderberry stems are excellent.
- Flames should be used for boiling and baking and coals for broiling and frying.
- Split wood burns better than whole chunks or logs.
- A log will burn in two; therefore, there is no need to chop it.
- Soft woods give more light than hard woods.
- Reflectors should be used for warmth.
- Fire tongs save scorched fingers.

4

Fig. 50. Water pockets—an easy-to-locate source of water

WATER

The Mountain West is often the scene of tragic experiences involving lack of water. But with a little luck and training anyone should be able to provide himself with enough drinking water to stay alive. There are areas, however, that require special equipment if water is to be secured, for much of the desert area of the Great Basin is devoid of running water. Sources can be located without too much trouble if a person knows how to look for them (Fig. 50).

Most of the moisture can be found on the sloping side of the hills in an area of dry mountain ranges. The other side is usually a steep escarpment and has faster runoff and less ground area for the collection of water. Narrow canyons and gullies should be followed up to their heads because small seeps and springs are often located nearby and run only a short distance before drying up.

The water table is usually close to the surface and one can locate it by digging:

■ At the base of cliffs and rocks where an abnormal amount of vegetation is thriving
■ In dry mudholes, sinks, riverbeds, and the bends of riverbeds, the latter usually providing the easiest source of water
■ At the base of large sand dunes on the shady or steep sides
■ Anywhere the ground is damp or muddy

45

Fig. 51. Drinking from a pool of water

Fig. 52. Finding water at a depth of 10 inches

■ In low spots where patches of salt grass, cattails, greasewood, willows, or elderberries grow.

Ore dumps and tailings indicate that water might be nearby in old mine shafts and pits.

Getting Water from the Soil

Obtaining water from the soil involves a few techniques with which a person who is going into the wilds should acquaint himself:

■ A hole dug in damp or muddy sink areas allows water to seep in and collect (Fig. 52).

■ Mud wrung in a shirt or other cloth will force out water.

■ An evaporation still—an invention developed by two American scientists, Dr. Ray D. Jackson and Dr. Cornelius H. M. van Bravel of the U.S. Department of Agriculture—involves some special equipment but is simple to construct (Fig. 53). A sheet of 6-by-6 foot clear plastic, a plastic drinking tube, and a container are all that are needed and can be included in a survival kit. A drinking tube is attached to the container—usually a bucket—and the bucket is placed into a 3-foot hole. Then a plastic sheet is stretched over the hole and held in place with dirt, which seals the hole off from the outside air. Next a rock is placed in the center of the plastic to weigh it down until it comes to within about 2 inches of the bucket. The drinking tube, fastened in the bucket, is arranged so that it extends outside the still.

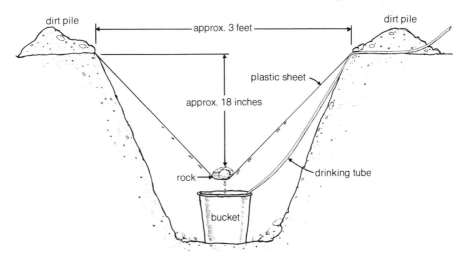

Fig. 53. Cross section of an evaporation still

Two of these stills in operation in even the driest deserts will produce enough water daily for one person. Green plants and sliced cactus placed in the pit will increase the amount of water. It is best to place the still in old riverbeds and in deep rich soil at the bottoms of gullies where moisture is most plentiful.

Some people have been unsuccessful in their attempts to secure water with an evaporation still. At least one group went public with their failures, suggesting that the principle was not sound. One look at their research examples, however, reveals that their methods were at fault, not the principle.

Collecting Water from the Air and from Plants

Water can also be extracted from almost any green vegetation by using a modified evaporation still. A large plastic bag is shaped according to the illustration (Fig. 54). This arrangement is limited to the amount of vegetation you can handle at one time, but may produce adequate supplemental water for survival. It is a good idea to crush and cut up the vegetation for quicker release of its moisture.

In many arid regions of the world primitive peoples supply themselves with water by arising before dawn to mop up the dew

Fig. 54. Modified evaporation still

Fig. 55. Dew available in early morning

from rocks and plants. A person using this technique in desert areas can gather a large supply of dew in the early morning (Fig. 55).

The easiest way to gather it is to use a handkerchief or a shirt to gently mop it up and then wring it into a container. If a handkerchief or other cloth is not available, a handful of dry grass will do the job. It is possible to mop up almost a quart an hour using this method.

Many plants and trees contain enough water to allay thirst, but getting it is a problem. A cactus can be cut and peeled and the moisture sucked out, but this is not the same as drinking running water; it is more like drinking Elmer's glue. However, larger cacti in the Southwest can be a good source of water when the tops are cut off and the center pulp mashed and stirred with a stick. The pulp can then be wrung to obtain the water.

Collecting Water from Water Pockets

In the Southwest much of the desert is made up of uplifted sandstone ridges or folds that sometimes run a hundred miles or more and completely dissect the land areas into separate valleys and drainages. These exposed areas of stone absorb very little moisture, and a light rainstorm or snowstorm can cause considerable runoff which in turn cuts deep channels and scoops out pockets in the surface. These pockets are numerous but extremely difficult to find, and as a result a person must ignore his basic instinct which causes him to look in the lower parts of a valley for water and

49

Fig. 56. Narrow canyons—source of water pockets

Fig. 57. Water pockets formed in sandstone

instead seek the high ground where the water pockets are located. The areas which one should carefully check are side canyons, narrow clefts, and especially white sandstone ridges (Fig. 56).

These hidden pockets may hold water for several months after a rain. In fact, some pockets are actually large tanks holding hundreds of gallons, while others are very small, holding only a few quarts (Fig. 57).

I have traveled with survival students as far as 200 miles on foot across southwestern deserts without a canteen, relying mostly on these water pockets and a few small springs and seeps. Some stretches, to be sure, were completely devoid of water, but by carefully studying the terrain and sandstone formations, we have always been able to prepare a route and cross these areas to water-pocket country on the other side.

Precautions in Using Water

A person inexperienced in the outdoors will want to be thrifty in his use of water and will benefit from a few precautions suggested here:

■ Nothing should be eaten if water is not available—eating uses up the body's water reserve.
■ Water should be stored in the stomach and not in a canteen; people have died from dehydration with water still in their canteens.
■ Water polluted by animals or mud tastes bad, but it is harmless if boiled.
■ Muddy water can be partially cleared by allowing it to stand overnight, run through several thicknesses of cloth or a grass filter, or seep through the bank into a hole dug about a foot away. If the water is brackish or salty the top 6 inches of salty soil between the hole and the source of water should be removed before the water is allowed to seep into the hole.
■ There should be no traveling during the heat of the day and walking should be done slowly, not in a hurry.
■ Such things as pebbles in the mouth, small sips of water, and chewing gum may relieve thirst, but they do not stop dehydration.
■ The drinking of blood or urine only increases dehydration of the body. But it helps to soak clothing in urine, as it cools the body during the evaporation process.

5

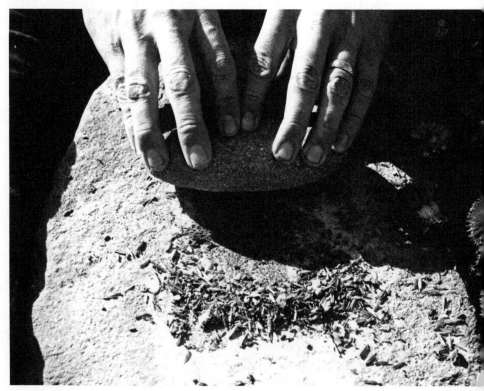

Fig. 58. Grinding sunflower seeds on a metate

PLANTS

The American West is certainly no Garden of Eden with respect to food plants, but the variety offered is extensive enough, and anyone with a good understanding of harvesting and preparation methods can live off these plant resources (Fig. 58).

It has been said that a person who can survive on the Great Basin can survive anywhere in the world. There are areas that surpass the hot barrenness of the Sahara, the cold ruggedness of Mongolia, and the jagged steepness of the Alps. But in all of these conditions nature has provided adequately for the trained survivor. The food quest is exacting and strenuous, and knowledge of the plant life is a must, inasmuch as so many edible species resemble poisonous ones. A careful study of these plants is essential.

Moreover, a person must be aware of the impact that one man can have on a wildland environment, especially on pristine desert lands. Some plants take several years to grow large enough to harvest, and one meal could require several plants, perhaps the number found in about an acre of land. For example, some plants are becoming rare as their habitats are being destroyed by agriculture and urbanization. One person could easily gather all the sego lily bulbs that occur in an acre or two of natural grassland for only one meal. Plants that have an annual crop of edible parts that can be harvested without injury to the plant should be used first. In other words, the trainee should exercise his "ecological conscience" and conserve whenever possible.

A certain amount of taste-bud training, which comes from experimentation and mental determination, is often necessary if one is to find some of the plants palatable. One should taste wild foods often and do so with a positive attitude. Many people die amid plenty simply because they cannot "stomach" wild foods; however, in these cases the stomach reacts only to the stimulus given by a prejudiced brain. Some people even develop defense mechanisms against eating certain foods. Needless to say, these defenses can kill even a healthy person lost in the wilds.

Harvesting Food Plants

Roots

Finding an edible root is fairly easy, but most roots grow deep, and digging them out can be difficult unless one is prepared with a few good techniques. Skillfully applied, a simple device called a digging stick saves time and energy that is otherwise expended scraping and grubbing with flat stones and fingers (Fig. 59). The stick is made from a stave of hardwood about three feet long and one inch in diameter. After the bark is removed the stick is hardened in the fire and the tip of it rubbed into a chisel shape on a coarse rock. Green wood hardens after about four or five scorchings in the fire, but several scorchings are required to drive out the sap. Care must be taken that the wood does not burn, for a good fire-hardened stick must be baked, not charred.

Digging down to a tasty root involves moving a lot of dirt, and the digger finds that it is easier if he makes the root come to him. He can do this by pushing the stick down alongside the plant until it is even with or below the root. Then by slightly prying, but mostly by lifting, he can flip the root to the surface (Fig. 60).

Seeds

When seeds are ripe they can be gathered in large quantities with a seed beater and a gathering basket. The seed beater is a small woven dish or ladle used to knock the ripened seeds from the plants. It should be dish-shaped so that it can catch and propel the seeds into the basket. The basket must be large enough to catch the seeds yet small enough to be held in one arm. A shallow woven tray is ideal, but a shirt held open with a willow hoop will also work.

Fig. 59. Digging wild onions with a digging stick

Fig. 60. Proper use of digging stick

Plants that form large amounts of seeds in clusters such as Amaranth (*Amaranthus*) need only be stripped with the hand for removal of the seeds. Flower seeds such as those of the nutritious sunflower (*Helianthus*) can be beaten from the head with a seed beater and also picked by hand or rubbed from the head on a flat stone (Fig. 61).

Preparing Food Plants

Roots

Flour from roots can be made by drying and grinding the roots on a metate in much the same manner as that used for seeds. A metate is a slab of rock that has been smoothed. Roots may be roasted whole and eaten like baked potatoes or mashed on a metate and eaten like mashed potatoes. Roasting, baking, or boiling may be used for most roots unless leaching is necessary. Leaching of bitter greens, roots, and nuts is done by boiling them in several changes of water or by pouring hot water through a bag of the

Fig. 61. Rubbing seeds from plant

Fig. 62. Lining a steaming pit with stones

mashed food. However, this process takes away much of the food value of plants and should be used only when the food is too bitter to be eaten otherwise.

A steaming pit is the most effective way to cook roots and greens, as well as meat and other foods. The pit is lined with stones and a fire is built in it. After an hour or more, the coals are scraped out and the pit is lined with wet green grass. The food is then placed on the grass and covered quickly with more wet grass. Next, water is poured on the food to induce steam, and the pit and its contents are quickly covered with flat rocks or a piece of cloth, canvas, or hide. Dirt is then heaped over the entire pit to seal in the steam, and the food is allowed to cook in the pit for several hours. One advantage of preparing food in this manner is that its flavor and nutritional value are saved (Figs. 62–64).

Roots and berries can be dried for future use. The roots are cooked and mashed into small flat cakes and then dried on flat rocks until hard. Berries must be partially dried first and then mashed into cakes for the final drying by being pounded in a

Fig. 63. Preparing the pit for grass and food

Fig. 64. Applying a dirt covering to the pit

mortar or they can be mixed with pounded meat for pemmican. However, these dried cakes must be broken up or ground before they are added to stew.

Seeds

Seeds must be threshed and winnowed if most of the chaff and stems are to be removed. One can accomplish this by beating the seeds with sticks and then tossing them on a winnowing tray, letting the wind blow away the chaff. This ancient method may seem rather crude, but it is effective under limited conditions. Seeds may also be tossed in a blanket or tossed into the air from a pile on the ground. A blanket or tray saves many of the tossed seeds from being lost in the dirt. One can winnow small amounts by taking a handful at a time and blowing away the chaff while he pours the seeds from one hand to the other (Figs. 65–67).

Fig. 65. Beating seeds

Fig. 66. Winnowing seeds by tossing

Most seeds are tastier and more nutritious when ground into flour or cracked for mush than when eaten whole. A most valuable method of making flour or cracking seeds involves a grinding stone. A handful of dry seeds is placed on a smooth stone (the metate) and ground with a mano or handstone (a loaf-shaped rock with one flat side). The handstone is held in the hands and rubbed back and forth on the metate with a pounding, scraping motion. It is best to work with the metate placed in the middle of a blanket to avoid losing seeds during the grinding process. Wet grinding may prove easier for some and is accomplished by dampening the seeds until they are soft and then grinding them into a dry paste (Fig. 68).

Seeds may also be dried or parched for preservation. The parching process is not difficult but requires a steady hand and a good parching tray. A tray can be made from willows woven

Fig. 68. Using a metate to grind seeds

Fig. 67. Winnowing seeds by handfuls

59

closely to form a large shallow bowl. A dishpan will also do. The bottom of the tray is covered with seeds and then a layer of hot hardwood coals is poured into it. The contents are stirred and the tray is shaken until all of the seeds are toasted. The hot coals are then flipped away and the contents of the tray are poured onto a flat rock or pan and cleaned by hand.

Dried seeds, roots, and berries can be safely stored in pits at the back of dry rock shelters and in crevices. A pit approximately two feet deep and lined with grass is sufficient. The dried food is placed in the pit and covered with dry sagebrush leaves and juniper bark, and then at least six inches of dirt is piled over all of this (Fig. 69). A pit made in dry dust and soil beneath an overhanging ledge will remain dry for years, and insects and rodents will rarely bother it.

Barks and Greens

Barks, leaves, and stems should be stripped and picked with care, and only the young tender portions should be selected. If possible, one should keep them fresh and cool while gathering them, but they must not be soaked in water to be kept fresh.

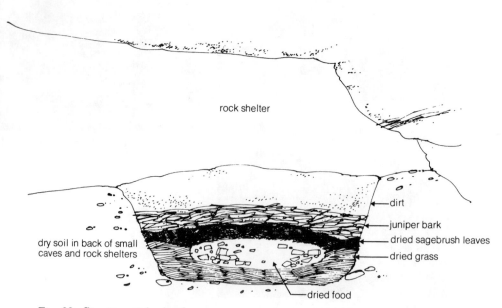

rock shelter

dirt

juniper bark

dried sagebrush leaves

dry soil in back of small caves and rock shelters

dried grass

dried food

Fig. 69. Storage pit for food

Geography of Plant Life

A knowledge of plant zones will help in the search for useful and edible species. Many useful varieties are found nearly everywhere the elevation and latitude are right, so one can apply these principles to nearly every temperate-to-arid region on the earth.

Topography determines the flora primarily through its effect upon precipitation and temperature. Altitude is more important in this respect than latitude. Generally, precipitation increases rapidly with altitude in semi-dry desert or plateau regions. This affects the amount and variety of plant growth in an area and will determine what to look for in the quest for food and tools.

Mountain structure also helps determine the water runoff patterns that affect plant life. A range that is a balanced anticline has equal runoff on opposite sides. Most ranges, however, are monocline with one steep escarpment and one gradual plane or dip (Fig. 70). On the steep side of the mountain the drainage area is small and the moisture flows down the steep rocky face, much of it sinking under the thick alluvial deposits forming valley floors. The water seldom emerges as springs.

The long axial side of a mountain range has more settled deposits and more land surface to collect and channel water. Springs, creeks, and damp areas are more frequent, favoring some species of plants, while the more arid steep sides of the mountains favor other types of plants.

Also, the slopes of hills facing in a direction that catches more direct sunlight will be more arid, while the opposite side of the hill,

Fig. 70. Monocline slope

where the sun's rays strike at a more shallow angle to the land surface, will have less evaporation. The snow stays longer on that side of the hill, and evergreens, shrubs, and larger species will thrive there.

Within a given area, one may be able to walk through several "life zones" in a day or perhaps several days. Each of these life zones contributes to human existence in a very different way and consequently predetermines to a large degree the movements of an informed survivor. The flora is most important. Also, the distribution of food animals depends somewhat upon the flora.

The floristic zones are related primarily with altitude, secondarily with latitude. The zones listed below are adapted and named solely as distinguishing factors so as to be more applicable over a broad range of the earth's temperate-arid zones.

Arctic-Alpine Zone

Above timberline, usually above 11,000 feet in altitude. In this limited environment the flora is restricted and scrubby and consists mainly of grasses. These are unimportant to man as food sources except as they support animal species which can be used by man, although some of the grass seeds are edible in season. Firewood is scarce and constructive materials are difficult to obtain due to the shortness and twisted nature of the wood. A survivor would quickly leave this area for a lower elevation if at all possible.

Canadian Zone: spruce-fir belt

9,000 to 11,000 feet. The trees include some species of fir, spruce, pine, and several willows.

There are about sixteen species of herbaceous grasses, most of which have seeds that will serve as food. The grasses may include wheat grass, redtop, bluegrass, and needlegrass.

There are about twenty other characteristic plants in this belt, of which only three are considered important food plants: gooseberry, wax currant, and elderberry. Other plant species can be used for greens and root foods, but these are scarce. Constructive plants are scarce and brittle, making shelter building and tool making difficult at best. About the only wood in this belt suitable for making tools for fire making is the willow, which at this altitude is considered a poor fire stick.

Canadian Zone: aspen-fir belt

7,000 to 9,000 feet. Trees include other species of fir, aspen, pine, and willow.

There is a great increase of edible grasses, greens, roots, and berries at this altitude. Some of them are strawberry, waterleaf, Indian potato, arrowleaf balsamroot, grasses, bracken fern, chokecherry, currant, elderberry, goldenrod, miner's lettuce, mints, mountain dandelion, mule's ears, mullein, nettles, onions, Oregon grape, plantain, raspberry, rose, salsify, sego lily, service-berry, docks, spring beauty, thistle, violet, wild hyacinth, yampa, yarrow, and yellow fritillary.

The number of constructive plants increases also, with the addition of sagebrush, ranging up from lower elevations, and several fiber-producing plants. Many useful woods for weapons, traps, and camp gear are available. This is still a difficult zone in which to survive indefinitely even under normal conditions, and one would be better off to move to a lower transitional zone.

Transitional Zone: mahogany or yellow pine belt

This intermediate zone is characterized by the blending of species from the zones above it with those of the zones below it, along with its own characteristic plants. This feature alone makes survival in this area superior. The characteristic trees are yellow pine and scrub mahogany. Some oak brush is present.

Nearly all the edible plants listed in the aspen-fir belt are found here, as well as those found in the upper reaches of the piñon-juniper belt.

Shelter, fire, and constructive resources are abundant and the weather is less severe in either extreme during most of the year.

Upper Sonoran Zone: piñon-juniper or artemisia belt

5,000 to 7,000 feet. This zone occupies the greater part of most mountain ranges and foothills and high valleys. Trees are piñon, juniper or cedar, cottonwoods, and many shrubs.

There are fewer species of edible plants, but in most cases the increase in volume of a single species more than compensates. Biscuit root, sego lily, camas, cattail, and other edibles are prolific and bulky, making harvesting easier. Chokecherry and currant berries ripen early. Many greens are present along watercourses. Notable species also include amaranth, arrowhead, beeplant, grasses, bulrush, burdock, burreed, ground cherry, heron's bill, horsetail, Indian ricegrass, lamb's quarter, mallow, mints, Mormon tea, mustards, plantain, prickly pear cactus, prickly lettuce, purslane, red clover, salsify, samphire, sorrel dock, sour dock, sunflower, thistle, and watercress.

Constructive plants include service berry, reedgrass, rose, sagebrush, greasewood, white willow, juniper, nettle, milkweed, dogbane, and sumac.

Aboriginal inhabitants spent most of their time in these belts, ranging upward only seasonally for special food sources.

Northward from the 42nd parallel, roots, tubers, and berries increase dramatically. In those areas, increased precipitation at lower altitudes produces many "prairies" which abound in food plants such as camas and bitteroot.

Lower Sonoran Zone: creosote-bush or covillea belt

This comprises warm, low valleys, mainly south of the 37th parallel. Here, in addition to plant forms found in other Sonoran belts, there are larger numbers of yucca and cactus species. The dominant edible plants include mesquite, screw bean, yucca, cactus, creosote bush, and Mormon tea.

This area is a more important food belt than the Arctic-Alpine Zone at the other end of the scale. Survivors depend more on the streams and oases for travel routes and usually find sufficient food sources along the waterways which range down from the higher artemisia belts.

Edible Plants*

The following list contains many of the more important food plants found in the Great Basin plateau areas of the western United States. In this rugged section of America the plant life is rather restricted and in most cases adapted to arid conditions. The higher elevations produce a wider variety of edible species which also grow in the desert valleys along stream courses. Edible seeds are the most common food source and comprise over half of the available species. I have supplied the location for only those plants

*Some plants which are edible are also poisonous unless prepared with caution; others are easily confused with poisonous plants. To aid the reader and to caution him, a † precedes each of these plants.

that grow in definite habitats. My intent is not to differentiate between native and introduced plants—if a plant grows in uncultivated areas, for my purposes here it is considered wild.

Note: In the following list of edible plants, the common name(s) is listed first, followed by the scientific—generic and species—name(s). Whenever the generic term (always capitalized and italicized) appears alone, usually many—and in some cases all—species of that genera are edible, but are too numerous to list. Whenever the species name (italicized, but not capitalized) is listed after the generic term, only that species is to be used. Each color photograph shown for a given plant is of only one species, but is usually one of the most common species of the given genera and is often representative of it.

Amaranth, Pigweed; *Amaranthus*

Description: Amaranth, an annual herb, has veiny alternate leaves and bears seeds which are black and grow in terminal or axillary clusters. (Colorplate 1, p. 185).

Preparation and Uses: Pigweed is known as America's forgotten cereal grain. Its shiny black seeds make a suitable cereal raw or cooked and may be added to soups, stews, and bread. The young leaves make a superior green when cooked like spinach soon after they are picked.

In late summer the seeds may be stripped from the stalk by hand or the whole plant can be pulled up. One can thresh the seeds by beating bundles of the stalks with a stick and winnowing the chaff as he tosses the contents in a blanket. The yield may amount to a pound or more of seeds from only a small armload of the plants.

Arrowhead, Wappato; *Sagittaria latifolia*

Description: Arrowhead grows in water or marshes and is easily identified by its deep green arrowhead-shaped leaves that protrude from the water or lie flat like a lily pad. The stalk is a single stem that bears fruit which grows from lateral spikes in the form of round heads containing flat seeds. The fibrous root system spreads directly from the tuft of the leaves and grows some distance into the shallow mud. In the late fall small tubers form on the rootstalks. (Colorplate 1, p. 185.)

Preparation and Uses: The small tubers, forming only in the late fall, can be gathered throughout the fall, winter, and early spring. One can harvest them by wading into the water and feeling in the mud with his toes or hands. He can often harvest large amounts by raking the water and mud to a depth of about six inches with a forked stick. This breaks the tubers from the roots so that they float to the surface. The only disadvantage to gathering arrowhead is that the weather is usually icy cold during the harvesting season and bare feet and arms suffer. In addition, one must be aware of conservation techniques; obviously an onslaught on streams or marshes may have a negative effect on the environment.

The tubers are roasted or baked to remove the stinging and poisonous properties. They taste something like potatoes, and can be baked, mashed into cakes, and dried for future use.

Arrowleaf Balsamroot, Balsamroot; *Balsamorrhiza*

Description: A member of the composite family, arrowleaf balsamroot is low growing and has arrow-shaped basal leaves and stems topped with yellow flowers that resemble sunflowers. (Colorplate 1, p. 185.)

Preparation and Uses: The large young root is edible when cooked. Some roots can be eaten raw but are bitter. The best way to prepare them is to pit steam large quantities for twenty-four hours or more and then mash and shape them into cakes for storage.

Asparagus; *Asparagus officinalis*

Description: Asparagus grows in moist ground near civilization. Its young shoots rise from the ground in the early spring and later become tall and branching and bear red berries. (Colorplate 2. p. 186.)

Preparation and Use: The young shoots can be eaten raw or cooked and prepared in the manner typical for domestic asparagus.

Beeplant; *Cleome*

Description: Beeplants are annual herbs with stems that are one to three feet tall. The leaves are branching with three leaflets, and the seed pods are one to two inches in length. The flowers are yellow or rose-purple, depending on the species. These plants grow mostly in sandy ground at lower elevations. (Colorplate 2, p. 186.)

Preparation and Uses: The greens can be eaten if they are boiled in two or three changes of water to remove the bitter taste. However, they are tastier when mixed with other foods after they are cooked. The cooked shoots can be dried and used as an emergency food. After the plant is cooked for several hours, the liquid serves as a black dye.

†Biscuit-root, Kouse; *Cymopterus*

Description: A member of the carrot family, biscuit-root consists of several edible species having swollen, bulblike roots. The plants grow on hillsides and in rocky places throughout the West and are often found in quite arid places. The flowers are borne on compound umbels and the leaves are divided into narrow segments like carrot leaves. Care should be taken not to confuse biscuit-root with related species that usually grow in damp areas and are often poisonous. This family should be studied carefully for identification of the various genera, some of which are deadly, such as the poison hemlock. (Colorplate 3, p. 187.)

Preparation and Uses: The seeds of some species are edible when ground into mush or flour. The root is a favored ingredient of stews and tastes something like dumplings. It can be boiled or roasted in a pit for best results, and if mashed and dried in cakes after it is cooked, it will keep indefinitely. This was the famous "bread of cows" (kouse) so eagerly sought by the Lewis and Clark expedition.

Blazing Star, Stickleaf; *Mentzelia*

Description: Blazing star is a coarse branching plant one to three feet tall, bearing beautiful yellow flowers and leaves covered with barbed hairs. Because of the barbed hairs the lance-shaped leaves often stick to clothing. The edges of the leaves are deeply cleft or pinnate. The root is buried deep as opposed to similar looking plants that have spreading root systems. Blazing star sometimes grows in seleniferous soils. (Colorplate 3, p. 187.)

Preparation and Uses: The seeds, after they are parched and ground into flour or meal, can be used as a serviceable but not too tasty food for mush and bread.

Bluegrass; *Poa* (Western)

Description: A grass common to rangeland, bluegrass bears seeds in narrow spreading seed heads. It is not too important to distinguish between the various grasses, as most that bear harvestable seeds in a grainlike husk are edible. (Colorplate 3, p. 187.)

Preparation and Uses: The seeds, if harvested with a seed beater, can be a good source of food when the season is right. But since most grass seeds drop shortly after maturity, the season is limited. Prepare seeds as you would any grain for soups, cereal, or bread.

†Bracken Fern; *Pteridium aquilinum*

Description: The most common of our ferns, bracken fern is coarse and covered with felty hairs at the base, and its young shoots uncurl in juicy stalks called fiddleheads (because of their resemblance in shape to the fiddle). The mature plant has a three-forked stem bearing light green fronds. (Colorplate 4, p. 188.)

Preparation and Uses: Young fiddleheads have long been a popular potherb in many countries. They are best when cooked like asparagus or when eaten raw with other foods. The mature fern is tough and unpalatable and may be toxic if eaten in large quantities. Under ordinary conditions, one should not uproot the plant for food. Some people are sensitive to the mature leaves.

Bristlegrass, Foxtail Millet; *Seteria*

Description: A grass with dense foxtail seed spikes which have long, stiff bristles, bristlegrass is a common species of wasteland and desert seeps. (Colorplate 4, p. 188.)

Preparation and Uses: The grain of this plant is similar to wheat or millet and is easily obtained by parching to remove the husks. The seeds ground for flour or boiled for cereal provide excellent nourishment.

Buffaloberry; *Shepherdia agentea, S. canadensis*

Description: A shrub or small tree, buffaloberry is somewhat thorny with oval or nearly oval leaves. Its small red berries last late into the fall.

Preparation and Uses: The berries are edible and can be cooked in stews or dried and pounded for meal and pemmican. The taste of the summer berries may be strange to some palates, but they are not poisonous as many people have assumed.

Bulrush; *Scirpus*

Description: Bulrush often grows taller than a man and has stems that are triangular in some species and round in others. A cluster of seeds grows at or near the tip. Bulrush grows along streams and marshes. (Colorplate 5, p. 189.)

Preparation and Uses: The rootstalks are edible and should be peeled and boiled or eaten raw. The center core of the root is especially tasty. The young shoots just protruding from the mud are a delicacy raw or cooked. One harvests them by wading into the water and feeling down along the plant until he comes to the last shoot in a string of shoots that protrudes above the water. He pushes his hands into the mud until he finds the lateral rootstalk. By feeling along the rootstalk in a direction leading away from the last shoot, one can often find a protruding bulb from which the new shoot is starting. This is easily snapped off and is edible on the spot. When the only available water is brackish and unfit to drink, these young shoots will allay thirst for a long time.

The rootstalks, when peeled, dried, and pounded into flour, make a good bread. This flour can also be mixed with a flour made from the seeds of the same plant. These are harvested by stripping and winnowing and are an important source of grain food.

The slender stalks are generally too tough for eating, but they are useful as material for cordage, sandals, baskets, and mats.

Burdock; *Arctium minus*

Description: Every farmer knows this bothersome weed. Burdock is characterized by large rhubarb-like leaves and purple flowers that produce a soft burr. The leaves are often over ten inches wide and a foot long and are smooth and velvety to the touch. The burrs are characterized by a mass of slender hooked spines that are not stiff. They cling to clothes and socks but seldom prick the skin. (Colorplates 5 and 6, pp. 189–190.)

Preparation and Uses: This useful plant has long been used in folk medicine for various external and internal complaints, generally as a tonic. The young leaves and shoots are edible when cooked as greens, and the root of the first-year plant is an excellent food when fried or roasted. If boiled, the root may be tough and strong unless the water is changed at least once.

The young stalks of the burdock can be peeled of their tough, bitter rind and the pithy center boiled for food. The roots can be dried and stored.

Burreed; *Sparganium*

Description: Aquatic plants with branching, leafy stems, the burreeds have small round seed heads resembling a burr located on the sides and near the top of the stalks. (Colorplate 6, p. 190.)

Preparation and Uses: The bulbous stem bases and tuberous roots of this plant are used for food in much the same way as cattails and bulrushes.

†Camas; *Camassia*

Description: Camas, a member of the lily family growing in damp meadows, is characterized by grasslike slender leaves radiating from the base. The stem is usually one or two feet tall and topped with a spike of blue flowers (Colorplates 6 and 7, pp. 190–191.) It should never be confused with the similar looking plant, death camas or *Zigadenus*, which is easily distinguished in appearance from camas by its smaller yellow or cream colored flowers. (Colorplate 7, p. 191.) Careless identification has caused the death of many wild plant eaters because the death camas is extremely poisonous. The common name, camas, should not be used as a guide to edibility, as *Veratrum* is also called camas and should be considered poisonous.

Camas should be harvested only when the plant is in bloom, for it is at this time that the survivalist can most easily distinguish it from the white or death camas. It can be harvested at other times of the year, but only by those who are very familiar with the plant's minute characteristics. It is possible after much observation of both plants to distinguish between them, both before and after flowering. Camas is never found growing in dry rocky ground as is the death camas; the flowers are blue, whereas the flowers of the death camas are smaller and yellow or cream colored; the leaf blades of most camas are slightly broader than those of most species of death camas; generally the bulbs of large mature camas are much larger than the largest bulbs of the death camas; camas grows mostly in the northern areas of the West: Idaho, Oregon, and Washington.

Preparation and Uses: The starchy bulb is an excellent food and can be gathered in large quantities with a digging stick. In meadows where these plants grow, a bushel of them can be gathered in a few hours. The bulbs are best prepared by being baked in a pit oven. After they are cooked, they can be mashed and dried in cakes for storage. Camas bulbs were an important source of food to many early Indian tribes.

Cattail; *Typha*

Description: Found along streams and marshes throughout the West, cattail has long bladelike leaves sometimes six feet long and a jointless stem terminating in a sausage-shaped seed head. (Colorplate 7, p. 191.)

Preparation and Uses: The cattail is an outstanding edible plant. The roots, young shoots, seed heads, and pollen are all edible, and the leaves make an excellent material for weaving. The down from the head makes a good insulation for blankets and sleeping bags.

The roots, when peeled and dried, can be made into flour for bread. One can also obtain the starch from the roots by mashing and soaking them in water and stirring the mixture vigorously. After they have been stirred, the roots should be removed and the water allowed to sit overnight or until all the starch settles to the bottom of the container. The water is them poured off and the starch used as dough for making bread.

The young shoots are excellent when eaten raw or boiled like asparagus. The centers of the older shoots can be eaten the same way but are not as good.

In the early summer the spikes at the top of the seed head form clusters of yellow colored pollen which is very light and fine. It can be stripped from the stalks with the fingers and put in tight containers or bags to be used as flour for bread. It is especially good when mixed with coarser grain flour.

Before the pollen appears, the green head is boiled and eaten like corn on the cob. When dry, the heads are burned, leaving only the tiny roasted seeds, which can be eaten as mush or ground for flour. A large quantity of cattail heads yields only a small quantity of seeds.

The down, stuffed between two blankets that have been sewn together, will give excellent insulation in cold weather; stuffed into shoes, it will help prevent frostbite.

The leaves, stripped and dried, can be used to make matting and other woven materials like sandals, baskets, blankets, and ponchos.

Chicory; *Cichorium intybus*

Description: Chicory leaves resemble the leaves of a dandelion, but the chicory stem is branching and stiff. In late summer, blue flowers appear on the stiff irregular stalks.

Preparation and Uses: The leaves are used for a potherb much the same as dandelions, and the roots are edible in emergencies.

†Chokecherry; *Prunus virginiana*

Description: Chokecherry, a tree or shrub, is easily recognized in the fall by its clusters of red-black cherries. The bark is reddish grey and somewhat speckled with lateral lines that resemble those on the bark of the domestic cherry tree. (Colorplate 8, p. 192.)

Preparation and Uses: The cherries of this tree are an excellent food despite the cyanogenetic poison contained in the seed. The cherries without the pits are puckery, but good raw. Cooked, they make an excellent jam. Slightly dried and crushed—seeds and all—on a mortar and dried in cakes, these berries provide nourishment that is lasting and satisfying. Before they are eaten, the dried cakes must be cooked to help drive off the poison from the seeds. Pemmican is made by mixing fat and pounded dried meat with the meal of chokecherries and sealing it in gut or molding it into round balls for preservation.

Cottonwood; *Populus*

Description: Large trees growing along streams at most elevations, the cottonwoods have rough grey bark and bear flowers in drooping catkins that are borne in broad disks. The buds of these trees are resinous, and the leaves are serrate with long petioles. (Colorplate 8, p. 192.)

Preparation and Uses: The buds and leaves often provide a honeydew made by aphids that is edible. It is scraped from the leaves or skimmed off the surface of the water in which the leaves have been boiled. The inner bark and the sap of the tree are also useful emergency foods.

Currant; *Ribes*

Description: A shrub three to ten feet tall, the currant has toothed leaves and berries forming in clusters. The berries are gold, red, or black. (Colorplate 9, p. 193.)

Preparation and Uses: The berries ripen early and provide excellent food which can be eaten fresh or dried. They may be prepared in any of the ways mentioned for chokecherries. None are known to contain poisonous principles, and they can be used in large amounts. The stems of currant make excellent arrow shafts.

†Elderberry; *Sambucus*

Description: Elderberry, a large shrub, is characterized by a large, pithy, brown colored stem bearing opposite compound leaves. The berries grow in flat-topped clusters and are deep purple when ripe. (Coloplates 9, p. 193.)

Preparation and Uses: The ripe berries in the fall are an important food and can be eaten raw or cooked. They keep well when dried and often lose their rank flavor. The flower clusters may be eaten dipped in a batter and fried or crushed into stew. The green leaves and stems of the plant are said to be poisonous. The pith of this plant is poisonous. The stems are important fire by friction materials.

Evening Primrose; *Oenothera*

Description: Evening primrose is either a low growing plant with large white flowers or a somewhat taller plant with yellow flowers. The low growing species is coarse with long leaves growing from the crown of the root. The taller species is rather stiff and erect and may appear to be prickly and coarse. The flowers of all the plants remain open during the night. (Colorplate 10, p. 194.)

Preparation and Uses: The seeds of various species can be eaten parched or ground into meal. Many of the species have bitter roots that are not very palatable, but some lose this property when dug in early spring and cooked. When made palatable, the roots are an important source of food in foothills and mountains.

Goldenrod; *Solidago*

Description: A tall plant with a long inflorescence crowded in a cluster and leaves that are often toothed, hairy, and alternate on the stem. (Colorplate 10, p. 194.)

Preparation and Uses: The seeds are used as thickening for stew. The young leaves and flowers make a potherb and tea.

Greasewood; *Sarcobatus*

Description: A stiff, light colored brush with spring shoots forming sometimes straight clusters of growth, grows in alkaline soils, usually near water sources. (Colorplate 10, p. 194.)

Preparation and Uses: The new spring tops are an edible source of salt. The wood is very hard and used for digging sticks, arrow foreshafts, trap trigger, and a variety of tools requiring a sharp point.

Ground Cherry, Husk Tomato; *Physalis*

Description: A low trailing plant, bears yellow flowers that later form in husks or bladders, containing a small fruit which resembles a tomato. The leaves of the plant are usually oblong and bluntly pointed. (Colorplate 11, p. 195.)

Preparation and Uses: The fruit may be eaten raw. It can be baked in ash cakes, cooked in stews, or made into jam.

Groundsel; *Senecio*

Description: Usually found in moist or wet meadows. The leaves are lance shaped, and dissected into narrow divisions, and its flowers are yellow. The plant is covered with tiny hairs that impart a grey sheen. The plant also contains a sticky sap. (Colorplate 11, p. 195.)

Preparation and Uses: The young leaves are edible as a potherb. They are also used to line cooking pits.

Hairgrass; *Deschampsia*

Description: A fine grass of higher altitudes. It is found in wet or damp soils. (Colorplate 11, p. 195.)

Preparation and Uses: The seeds may be harvested with a seed beater and ground for mush and flour.

Heron's Bill, Storkbill; *Erodium cicutarium*

Description: An herb which may form rosettes and later have spreading stems, heron's bill bears rose to lavender flowers. The seed resembles the stork's bill. These plants grow in open dry ground throughout the West. (Colorplate 12, p. 196.)

Preparation and Uses: The young plants are cooked for greens or eaten raw as salad.

Horsetail, Scouring Rush, Joint Grass, Snake Grass;
Equisetum

Description: Horsetail is the common joint grass so eagerly sought after by children for playthings. The stems are of two kinds: one is sterile and has many branches; the other is fertile and has no branches. The grass is jointed and pulls apart easily, and at the top of the fertile plant is a brown head. (Colorplate 12, p. 196.)

Preparation and Uses: The young shoots in the spring can be used as a potherb. Later the shoots become too stiff and contain a silica that gives them the name "scouring rush." They can then be used for cleaning metal, for polishing and honing bone implements and wooden shafts, and for sharpening pocketknives.

Indian Potato; *Orogenia linearifolia*

Description: Indian potato is a tiny plant with basal leaves that are divided into slender leaflets that look like bird tracks. The stem arises from a deep nutlike bulb, and the tiny white flowers grow in compound umbels. (Colorplate 13, p. 197.)

Preparation and Uses: This was a favorite of the Indians, who used it frequently for food. The bulb can be boiled, steamed, roasted, or baked in any of the ways used for preparing potatoes. However, the tiny bulbs are also tasty when eaten raw. They may be cooked and mashed into cakes for drying. They keep indefinitely when protected from moisture. The hard cakes can then be soaked and cooked in stew or soup. One of the tastiest roots found in the West, this plant grows in meadows and on mountainsides at higher altitudes.

†Indian Ricegrass; *Oryzopsis hymenoides*

Description: Indian ricegrass has slender stems and flat or in-rolled leaves and a tufted seed head which contains large grains. This plant is found on sand dunes and desert areas. (Colorplate 13, p. 197.)

Preparation and Uses: The seeds are ground for cereal. This grain is abundant and easily harvested. Seed heads containing black seeds should be discarded as they may have a harmful fungus infection.

Jerusalem Artichoke, Sunflower; *Helianthus tuberosus*

Description: A species of sunflower introduced from the Midwest and found growing in waste areas, jerusalem artichoke is usually more slender than the native sunflower of the West. It has large potatolike roots in the fall. (Colorplate 14, p. 198.)

Preparation and Uses: The large tuber is edible and formed an important food for the Indians of the Midwest. It has largely escaped cultivation in the West and is not generally found in unsettled areas.

Juniper, Cedar; *Juniperus*

Description: Evergreen shrubs or trees with blue berries, junipers are very common in the foothills and desert portions of the West. (Colorplates 14 and 15, pp. 198–199.)

Preparation and Uses: The blue berries of the junipers are bitter but nutritious and can be eaten in an emergency. If they are pounded and boiled, some of the bitter taste is removed. The inner white bark, stripped and pounded into a meal, will hold off starvation for a time.

Lamb's Quarter, Goosefoot; *Chenopodium*

Description: Lamb's quarter is a common weed of wastelands and stream banks. The leaves vary from ovate to lanceolate in the various species, and its seeds form in clusters. (Colorplate 15, p. 199.)

Preparation and Uses: The leaves and stems are edible when young. They can be eaten as salad or cooked like spinach. The seeds are also edible; they are ground into flour and used for making bread when mixed with other grain flour.

Mallow, Cheese Weed; *Malva*

Description: Annual plants with thick roots and stems that run along the ground, mallows bear small white to pale blue flowers. The fruit is round and flattened into the shape of a cheese wheel, hence the name *cheesies*. These plants are found around cultivated areas. (Colorplate 15, p. 199.)

Preparation and Uses: Mallows can be used as a potherb, and the leaves and stems may be cooked in soups. The fruit is excellent eaten raw or cooked, and the dried leaves make a superior warm drink.

Mannagrass; *Glyceria*

Description: Mannagrass has long narrow leaves and a long seed head. It is often found growing on stream banks and around seeps, and its long leaves sometimes hang into the water and float.

Preparation and Uses: The seeds are gathered with a seed beater, winnowed to remove the chaff, and used as a thickening for stews and soups. They can be ground on a metate for flour. Mannagrass is one of the better tasting grains that are found growing in the West.

Maple, Box Elder; *Acer negundo*

Description: A tree with leaves composed of three to five separate leaflets and winged seeds, the box elder is common to mountain valleys and gullies. (Colorplate 16, p. 200.)

Preparation and Uses: The winged seeds are roasted and eaten. Pounded for flour, the inner bark serves as an emergency food. When the sap rises in late winter, the sweet sap can be boiled down into a good maple syrup.

†Milkweed; *Asclepias syriaca*

Description: The stout stems of milkweed bear opposite entire leaves with broad midribs, and when broken, the stems and leaves emit a milky sap. The large pods, formed after flowering, bear seeds that are plumed with silky fibers. (Colorplate 16, p. 200.)

Preparation and Uses: Some milkweeds are highly poisonous. However, if a person carefully distinguishes *Asclepias syriaca* milkweed from the deadly dogbane, which is a similar plant, the young shoots of the former can be cooked and eaten. The very young seed pods can be boiled and eaten also. The sap may be heated for chewing gum and the fibers of the stalk used to make cordage and fish line.

Miner's Lettuce, Indian Lettuce; *Montia*

Description: Indian lettuce is a small succulent plant with round, fleshy leaves. Some of the leaves are joined to each other on both sides in such a way as to form a rounded disk or cup. (Colorplate 16, p. 200.)

Preparation and Uses: This tasty plant is the rival of garden lettuce for salads and raw greens and can be eaten in large quantities. When mixed with water cress and placed between two hotcakes made of Indian potato root dough, it is unexcelled for flavor and constitutes a rare and satisfying sandwich.

Mint; *Mentha* and other genera

Description: Members of the mint family are characterized by a square stem and opposite leaves. (Colorplate 17, p. 201.)

Preparation and Uses: Catnip, peppermint, horehound, spearmint, horsemint, sage, thyme, hyssop, and several other plants of the mint family are used for food and drink. As drinks, some are unmatched for their soothing qualities and often relieve headache, nausea, colic, and other nervous upsets that may be encountered in the wilds. The seeds can also be eaten or added to the leaves for steeping.

Mormon Tea, Brigham Tea, Squaw Tea; *Ephedra*

Description: A shrub with stiff, green colored, jointed branches and scale-like leaves, Mormon tea is found in the southern portions of the West and is easily identified. (Colorplate 18, p. 202.)

Preparation and Uses: The green stems can be steeped for a soothing drink, but the beverage may stain the teeth if used regularly.

Mountain Dandelion, False Dandelion; *Agoseris*

Description: Mountain dandelion looks like the common dandelion with its yellow flower; however, its leaves may or may not be toothed. (Colorplate 18, p. 202.)

Preparation and Uses: The leaves and roots are edible when cooked. The hardened sap or juice from the root and stems is also edible and can be used as chewing gum.

Mule's Ears; *Wyethia*

Description: *Wyethia amplexicaulis* has flower heads which resemble those of the sunflower. They are bright or orange yellow, and several heads grow on a stalk. The plant itself grows low to the ground, and its leaves are erect and glossy. *Wyethia helianthoides* is similar in appearance, having white flowers and a sticky, hairy stalk. These two species of mule's ears often cross-produce hybrids which bear yellow flowers on their hairy stalks. (Colorplate 18, p. 202.)

Preparation and Uses: The seeds are edible, and the roots of *Wyethia helianthoides* can be eaten after they are cooked for at least thirty hours in a steaming pit. Even then some people have to hold their noses to get it down.

Mustard, Shepherds Purse, White top, Peppergrass;
Sisymbrium, Brassica, Lepidium, and other genera

Description: These common mustards of every barnyard and of wasteland are evident in several forms. They are generally a leafy weed, erect with yellow or white flowers. The leaves are often deeply cleft. (Colorplates 19 and 20, pp. 203–204.)

Preparation and Uses: The seeds of all the species are edible, as well as the young greens which are eaten as a potherb.

Nettle, Stinging Nettle; *Urtica*

Description: Nettle is an erect plant with opposite toothed leaves that are long and pointed at the outer end. The stalks, stems, and leaves are covered with fine stinging hairs that are well known to most picnickers. (Colorplate 20, p. 204.)

Preparation and Uses: The leaves and young stems are edible as cooked greens. They are gathered with gloves or with large mullein leaves (*Verbascum*) used as pads for the hands. The stinging properties leave when the plant is cooked. The dried stalks in the fall are a source of excellent fibre for cordage.

†Oak; *Quercus*

Description: Oak ranges all the way from a shrub six inches high to the small common scrub oak which grows in the mountains to the large tree which grows in fertile valleys. *Q. Gambelli* is the most important. (Colorplate 20, p. 204.)

Preparation and Uses: The acorn can serve as an emergency food but must be leached of its tannic acid before it is eaten. The wood is used for digging sticks and bows.

†Onion, Wild Garlic, Nodding Onion; *Allium*

Description: Resembling the domestic onions, these small wild onions and garlics always have the familiar onion smell when their leaves are bruised. Plants looking like onions but lacking the characteristic smell should be checked closely, as some species such as death camas (*Zigadenus*) are very poisonous. Late in the season one can find this small onion plant by first finding the stalk. The dried flower head on the stalk looks like a white ball against the ground. (Colorplate 21, p. 205.)

Preparation and Uses: The whole plant is edible raw or cooked and is an excellent addition to any dish.

Oregon Grape, Algerita; *Mahonia*

Description: Oregon grape is a shrub with hollylike leaflets which grows low to the ground in dense thickets and under trees. Its leaves are spined and dark green. In the Southwest, other species often form large bushes or even trees bearing palatable fruit. (Colorplates 21 and 22, pp. 205–206.)

Preparation and Uses: The deep purple or red berries are edible raw or cooked and are rather tasty and tart. They can also be dried for future use. The root makes a superior yellow dye.

Piñon Pine; *Pinus monophylla, P. edulis*

Description: An evergreen tree which grows in many areas of the West, the piñon pine is characterized by its spreading growth and dense covering of pine cones containing large seeds. The cones of most pine trees do not bear these large seeds. (Colorplate 22, p. 206.)

Preparation and Uses: The cones are gathered and charred in a fire. In this way the seeds are roasted and loosened. Then they are beaten from the cones and used as one of the most important foods available in nature. They may be eaten shelled or ground up, shell and all, on a metate.

Plantain; *Plantago major, P. lanceolata*

Description: Plantain, a common lawn pest, grows in two varieties. *Plantago major* has flat leaves and *Plantago lanceolata,* long lance-shaped leaves, both of which are dark green and ribbed. The seed heads grow in dense clusters at the end of long stems. The whole plant is only about eight inches tall. (Colorplate 22, p. 206).

Preparation and Uses: The young leaves can be eaten and are also an important herb for dressing wounds (see Medicinal Plants, p. 89).

Prickly Lettuce, Wild Lettuce; *Lactuca*

Description: A common weed, prickly lettuce is characterized by several species, most of them having narrow leaves that are lobed. The plant bleeds a milky juice when injured. (Colorplate 23, p. 207.)

Preparation and Uses: The young leaves are edible when cooked, and the gum of the roots is made into chewing gum.

†Prickly Pear Cactus; *Opuntia*

Description: The prickly pear cacti have pear-shaped pads and fruits, and large patches grow on hillsides and deserts throughout the West. Many other cacti are edible but should be identified before they are eaten. (Colorplates 23 and 24, pp. 207–208.)

Preparation and Uses: The fruits and new joints of this plant should be scorched or peeled. They can be eaten raw or cooked, and the seeds can be ground into flour. Some cacti may be over a hundred years old; care should be used so as not to destroy them.

Purslane; *Portulaca oleracea*

Description: A small weed growing low to the ground, purslane has smooth, fleshy leaves with rounded ends and stems that are usually rose colored and juicy. (Colorplate 24, p. 208.)

Preparation and Uses: The whole plant is edible as a salad green or as a potherb.

†Rabbitbrush; *Chrysothamnus*

Description: Rabbitbrush, a stiff light colored brush with new green stems at the top, grows in alkaline soils, usually around water holes and lakes. (Colorplate 24, p. 208.)

Preparation and Uses: Rabbitbrush is poisonous to livestock. However, the secretion at the top of the roots can be chewed for gum.

Raspberry, Thimbleberry, Black Capa; *Rubus*

Description: All species are shrubs, some having spines with red, black, purple, blue, or orange berries, and all belong to the rose family. The common wild raspberry is perhaps the most prevalent. (Colorplate 25, p. 209.)

Preparation and Uses: The berries are edible in season and can be dried for future use.

Red Clover; *Trifolium*

Description: These wild red clovers resemble the domestic variety with its round flower head and three leaves. (Colorplate 25, p. 209.)

Preparation and Uses: The seeds are edible as well as the greens, and the steeped leaves and flowers are reputed to be good for colds and coughs.

Reed, Reed Canary Grass; *Phragmites communis*

Description: Long jointed and stout with hollow stems, reed resembles cane or bamboo. (Colorplate 25, p. 209.)

Preparation and Uses: The seeds are edible when cooked as cereal. The roots may also be eaten when cooked, and the young shoots eaten raw or cooked. The plant's main value is its use in weaving and in the manufacturing of arrow shafts.

Rose, Wild Rose; *Rosa*

Description: Every camper knows this thorny bush. This rose is similar to the domestic rose bush and usually has reddish colored stems bearing bright red fruit that matures in the fall after the first frost. (Colorplate 26, p. 210.)

Preparation and Uses: The rose hips or berries are a ready supply of nutritious food that lasts through the fall and often all winter. They are easily picked and ground on a metate for a meal or for flour, but the fresh fruit is also good when cooked. The numerous seeds are hard and must be cracked or ground before they are eaten. Rose hips contain a massive dose of Vitamin C and are very nourishing. The stems of the plant are the best arrow shafts.

Salsify, Oysterplant, Goatsbeard; *Tragopogon*

Description: The leaves of salsify are grasslike and slightly hairy, giving them a queer translucent appearance around the edges. The second-year plants produce yellow or purple flowers that later form large seed heads with umbrellalike fluffs that carry the seeds away in the wind. (Colorplates 26 and 27, pp. 210–211.)

Preparation and Uses: The first-year roots are edible when cooked, but as the first-year plant produces only leaves without flowers, it is often hard to recognize. The root of the second-year plant tastes like steamed oysters and is a rich wilderness food.

Samphire; *Salicornia*

Description: Small, light green, and branching, samphire has fleshy stems reaching up like claws and is found in saline bogs and marshes. (Colorplate 27, p. 211.)

Preparation and Uses: The plant is edible raw or cooked and is a rich source of salt. Added to stew, it provides all the salt flavoring necessary.

Sego Lily; *Calochortus*

Description: The small grasslike leaves of the sego lily grow among brush and trees in the foothills. Later a stem appears bearing a lovely yellow, creamy white, or bluish flower with light purple splotches at the base of the petals. As it is the state flower of Utah, it should be harvested only in emergencies or for scientific purposes. At one time the plant was thought to be almost extinct; it now grows abundantly in many areas although much less widespread than formerly. Some of the plants do not bloom, which often leads the layman to believe that this species is rare. (Colorplate 27, p. 211.)

Preparation and Uses: The tender bulb, harvested with a digging stick, is unsurpassed in flavor when roasted or boiled and can also be cooked and mashed into cakes for preservation.

Serviceberry; *Amelanchier*

Description: The serviceberries, shrubs or small trees, have simple leaves and blue colored fruit that resembles tiny apples when ripe. (Colorplate 28, p. 212.)

Preparation and Uses: The berries may be cooked or dried, mashed into cakes for drying, or mixed with dried meat for pemmican. The wood makes digging sticks, arrow foreshafts, and round bows.

†Sour Dock, Sorrel, Curly Dock, Yellow Dock, Wild Rhubarb, Indian Tobacco; *Rumex*

Description: The stems of sour dock are grooved, resembling rhubarb, and the flowers grow in clusters and form large seed clusters that turn brown in the fall. (Colorplate 28, p. 212.)

Preparation and Uses: If chopped and then boiled for a long time into syrup, the stems are especially good. If not too bitter, they may be eaten raw like rhubarb, but the leaves may be toxic if they contain too much oxalic acid.

Spring Beauty; *Claytonia lanceolata*

Description: A tiny plant, spring beauty is found in wooded areas and grows from a round nutlike corm. Its small white or pink flowers bloom early in the spring, and its leaves grow opposite on the stem in one pair. (Colorplate 29, p. 213.)

Preparation and Uses: An important source of food in the spring, the small bulbs are dug with a digging stick and can be prepared in any of the ways used to prepare potatoes. They also preserve readily after they are cooked and mashed into cakes for drying.

Strawberry, Wild Strawberry; *Fragaria americana*

Description: This strawberry is like the domestic variety, only smaller. (Colorplate 29, p. 213.)

Preparation and Uses: The berry is eaten in season and the leaves are steeped for an excellent hot drink.

Sumac, Squawbush; *Rhus trilobata*

Description: Sumac is a sprawling shrub with a three-lobed leaf or with three leaflets to a leaf that has broad outer ends; its berries form in clusters and are very sticky. (Colorplate 29, p. 213.)

Preparation and Uses: The berries serve as an emergency food and an even better drink. Steeped in water and drunk cold, they are very refreshing. The stems of the plant make the best material for weaving baskets.

Sunflower; *Helianthus*

Description: This is the common sunflower easily recognized by almost anyone. It has flowers in a large yellow head and rather prickly, hairy stalks. (Colorplate 30, p. 214.)

Preparation and Uses: The seeds of sunflowers are perhaps the most nourishing food found in the wilds. Harvested with a seed beater and then ground on a metate, they are used as mush. They should not be cooked, but just heated or eaten cold. They also make an excellent baby food; the Indians depended on them to a great extent for that purpose.

Thistle; *Cirsium*

Description: Many species of thistle exist, but generally they all may be described as succulent plants with many spines on the leaves and stems. (Colorplate 30, p. 214.)

Preparation and Uses: The young tender plant stems can be peeled and eaten, and the first-year roots are good when boiled with other food.

Thornapple, Haw, Hawthorn; *Crataegus*

Description: Thornapple is the only native tree with thorns of any size. It looks somewhat like an apple tree, its fruit resembling miniature apples.

Preparation and Uses: The berries are good food when dried and made into cakes. The dried cakes, ground and mixed with pounded jerky, make pemmican.

Umbrella Plant, Trumpet Plant, Wild Buckwheat; *Eriogonum*

Description: The leafless stalks of umbrella plant are topped by compound umbels of tiny yellow or cream colored flowers, and the stem arises from a dense cluster of leaves which are matted on the ground. The leaves are usually lance shaped and are white on the bottom side. The plant grows in open areas of dry soil up to 9,000 feet. (Colorplate 30, p. 214.)

Preparation and Uses: The leaves are cooked for greens, and the seeds are edible after they are ground on a metate into meal or into flour for making bread.

Violet, Dogtooth, Glacier Lily; *Erythronium grandiflorum*

Description: In spite of its name, violet is not a violet but a lily with a yellow flower and two large shiny oblong leaves arising from the base. The petals are very recurved, and the bulb is deep and rounded. The plant grows at higher altitudes along streams and in shaded woodlands. (Colorplate 31, p. 215.)

Preparation and Uses: The bulb is dug with a digging stick but is difficult to obtain because it grows so deep. The bulbs are excellent when cooked like potatoes, and they can also be cooked and mashed for storage. In addition, the leaves are edible as greens. The violet is a rare plant and should be used only in emergencies.

Watercress; *Nasturtium officinale*

Description: Green and leafy and growing in clear water, watercress has white threadlike roots that form thick mats along the edges of streams. The leaves of this plant have three to nine segments. Watercress also bears tiny white flowers. (Colorplate 31, p. 215.)

Preparation and Uses: Watercress, which has a pleasant tangy taste, is a favorite salad plant used raw as greens. Watercress and miner's lettuce, wrapped together in tortillas made from root flour, make an excellent wilderness sandwich. Watercress is the host plant for liverflukes, so it should be harvested only in water that is unaffected by livestock.

Waterleaf; *Hydrophyllum*

Description: The delicate waterleaf grows at higher altitudes on damp hillsides among dense growth of brush and trees. Its flower is a globular head of tiny white or purple flowers, and its leaves are broad, fleshy, and deeply divided, with rounded tips. (Colorplate 31, p. 215.)

Preparation and Uses: The whole plant is edible. The root-stalks, which are several tiny brown carrotlike appendages radiating from the base of the stem, make excellent stew and the plant tops serve as greens.

Wheat Grass, Blue Joint Grass, Quack Grass; *Agropyron*

Description: This is the common wheat grass and other similar species that are found throughout the West. It has a wheatlike seed head that contains a nutritious grain.

Preparation and Uses. The seeds are harvested with a seed beater and ground on a metate. They can be gathered in goodly amounts with a little patience. The rootstalks of this plant are also edible.

†Wild Hyacinth; *Brodiaea*

Description: Wild hyacinth has slender basal leaves and flowers—usually blue—that grow in clusters forming umbels. It is easily confused with camas or wild onions when not in bloom. Also the name *hyacinth* is misleading, for domestic hyacinth is poisonous. (Colorplate 32, p. 216.)

Preparation and Uses: The bulb, an important food source in higher elevations, is best cooked and eaten with greens or mashed and dried for future use in stews. Harvesting it with a digging stick is difficult because it grows deep.

Wild Rye; *Elymus*

Description: A common bunch grass seen along roadsides and in deserts, wild rye is tall and coarse. The plants are characterized by their flat leaves, and they bear a single erect spike of seeds at the end of each stem.

Preparation and Uses: The seeds are harvested by stripping or with a seed beater. Carefully winnowed, they make an excellent grain for mush and flour if the chaff is singed.

†Yampa, Wild Caraway; *Perideridia*

Description: A slender plant, yampa grows on damp hillsides and meadows in the foothills of the plateau area. The leaves are compound with narrow grasslike leaflets and usually dry up by flowering time. The flowers are borne in small white compound umbels. This plant is a member of the carrot family and positive identification is necessary before it is eaten. Typically, fruit is required for positive identification.

Preparation and Uses: The small fingerlike roots grow deep and sometimes form in groups of two or three. Perhaps some of the most important and tastiest roots found, they far outrank potatoes in flavor, and can be cooked in any of the ways used for potatoes. When cooked and mashed into cakes for drying, they keep a long time.

Yellow Fritillary, Yellowbell; *Fritillaria pudica*

Description: The small yellow fritillary has lanceolate, basal leaves and a single yellow or golden flower that hangs either sideways or down from the bent stalk. The root is a corm with a cluster of tiny rice-like bulblets surrounding it. The plant grows among the brush on damp hillsides. (Colorplate 32, p. 216.)

Preparation and Uses: The corm is edible, as are the rice-like bulblets and when cooked, they resemble rice in both appearance and taste. The green seed heads can also be eaten after they are cooked.

Medicinal Plants

Plants are necessary not only as food but also as mild medicine. The following plants have proved most helpful to people who have suffered from minor irritations, wounds, and burns while in the wilds.

Biscuit-root, Kouse; *Cymopterus*

The old roots of biscuit-root are an effective insecticide when boiled. Sprinkle the tea around camp and in sleeping areas. (Colorplate 3, p. 187.)

Burdock; *Arctium minus*

The young roots of the first-year burdock dug in early spring or late fall are often used as a salve or wash for burns, wounds, and skin irritations. (Colorplates 5 and 6, pp. 189–190.)

Cattail; *Typha*

The white starchy roots of the cattail have been pounded and mixed with animal fat and used as a salve in dressing burns. (Colorplate 7, p. 191.)

Chokecherry; *Prunus virginiana*

The inner bark of chokecherry has sometimes been used as a tea to check diarrhea. (Colorplate 8, p. 192.)

Mullein; *Verbascum thapsus*

The burned leaves of mullein, used as an incense, has been used in relieving lung congestion. (Colorplate 19, p. 203.)

Nettle, Stinging Nettle; *Urtica*

The root and leaves of nettle, when drunk as a tea, has been used for stopping diarrhea, but can cause constipation. (Colorplate 20, p. 204.)

Onion, Wild Garlic, Nodding Onion; *Allium*

The smashed leaves of wild onions, rubbed on the arms and neck, are an effective insect repellent. However, the leaves, because of their offensive odor, are also a very effective people repellent. (Colorplate 21, p. 205.)

Peppermint; *Mentha piperita*

Peppermint is an aromatic stimulant and has been used to relieve nausea, colic, nervous headache, and heartburn.

Pines; *Pinus*

The pitch of the lodgepole pine has been used for disinfecting and protecting open sores. The young shoots of the western white pine are boiled and used as cough syrup or as a mild drink for treating coughs and upset stomachs.

Plantain; *Plantago*

The fresh leaves of plantain act as a mild astringent when mashed to a pulp and applied to cuts and other wounds. (Colorplate 22, p. 206.)

Rose, Wild Rose; *Rosa*

Very rich in vitamins A and C, wild rose "hips" are used as a tea or eaten raw. (Colorplate 26, p. 210.)

Serviceberry; *Amelanchier*

The boiled green inner bark of service berry has been used for an eyewash. (Colorplate 28, p. 212.)

Sour Dock; *Rumex crispus*

The roots of curly dock have been smashed and used for a poultice on sores and swellings. (Colorplate 28, p. 212.)

Sweet Flag; *Acorus calamus*

The root of sweet flag, when steeped and drunk as a tea, has been used to relieve upset stomach.

Yarrow; *Achillea millefolium*

The leaves of yarrow are often used to stop bleeding in wounds, to reduce inflammation, and to heal rashes when applied directly to the wounded area. They are also used for tea and for relief of toothache when chewed. (Colorplate 32, p. 216.)

Directions for Gathering Botanicals

■ Leaves of biennials are most valuable during their second year of growth. Leaves should always be collected in clear dry weather in the morning after the dew is off and are at their best when the plant is in bloom.

■ Flowers are worth more medicinally if used as soon as they open.

■ Bulbs and roots are more useful if gathered at the time the leaves of the plant die in the autumn.

■ Only the inner bark, preferably gathered in the fall, should be used.

6

Fig. 71. Hunting and killing—justified only by sincere need

ANIMALS

Animal life is an important and substantial source of food for survival. But the hunting and trapping of animals for that purpose and for other needs, such as clothing and tools, requires a great deal of prowess and patience. One must be trained in order to be a good hunter and trapper, and he must observe a certain code of conduct during that training. All life, from a tiny insect to a hot-tempered moose, has a sacred right to fulfill the measure of its creation and in no way does this fulfillment require that a beast become sport for man. Hunting for existence is a different proposition altogether and reflects a more serious and mature relationship with nature. Hunger is humbling and killing creates a void in the earth that is justified not by a shelf laden with trophies but rather by sincere need (Fig. 71).

Hunting an animal is a challenge, and if a need for the animal is present, one can certainly enjoy that challenge. However, need implies putting the animal to good use; in other words every part of it should be used for survival. To waste even a shred is inexcusable.

The methods used to obtain game in a primitive situation are varied, but many are cruel and should be avoided unless no other means presents itself.

Every resource for gathering in meat must be considered and used. If one puts all of his effort into hunting larger game, he usually ends up with only an empty stomach. Therefore, trapping small game and harvesting insects are a must in most areas. Hunting, then, should be second nature to the survivor, but it should not receive the main emphasis.

Insects

Some insects provide a life-saving source of food in an emergency and can often be found in profusion after a hatch. If properly harvested, they can insure a food supply for several days. On the other hand, a survivor may have to be content with an occasional grub to add to his stew. When he forages, he should never disregard the lowly grasshopper because he thinks it is too insignificant to matter. The nutritional value of insects is high and adds substantially to a meager diet. However, *all insects must be cooked,* as they harbor internal parasites that are very harmful to human beings.

One must be careful not to expend more energy harvesting food than that which the food can replace. In particular, catching insects such as grasshoppers can become exasparating and tiring unless one learns a few tricks.

Listed here are some of the more common insects which provide good food. Also listed are appropriate methods of harvesting them and uses to which they can be put.

Grasshoppers, Locusts, Crickets, and Katydids,
Orthoptera

Uses: If there are enough of these insects, they can be roasted and dried, ground into meal, and served in soups and stews. Small amounts can be boiled or roasted and served whole in soups or stews.

Harvesting Methods: At night grasshoppers climb tall plants and cling to the stalks near the top and can be picked from the plants early in the morning while they are chilled and dormant. When grasshoppers are located in large quantities, several people can drive them with switches to one side of a meadow or clearing. The grasshoppers can then be caught as they are swatted with willow switches. Grasshoppers and locusts in large amounts are available in some locales from late July until late August, usually in mountain meadows and plateau regions of the West.

Stone flies and other nymphs, *Plecoptera*

Uses: Nymphs can be boiled in soups and stews with other food.

Harvesting Methods: Nymphs inhabit the undersides of stones in fast-moving streams and crawl on the water's edge in the early spring. They are simply picked from the stones and grass stems and stored in a wet container until they are needed for cooking.

Cicadas, *Homoptera*

Uses: The wings of the adult cicada are plucked, and then the insect is boiled in stew.

Harvesting Methods: Cicadas are found in juniper trees and brush in desert regions and can be harvested in the early morning in the same manner as that used for grasshoppers. Cicadas can be located when they make a loud clicking noise somewhat similar to the sound of rattlesnakes.

Ants, *Hymenoptera*

Uses: Ants in quantity may be roasted, ground into powder, and used as an addition to soups and stews. When the ants are roasted, the abdomen usually separates from the rest of the body and can be winnowed to produce a sweet black sugar.

Harvesting Methods: Carpenter ants are found in dead trees and stumps and may be gathered by hand as they are quite large. Small red and black ants build rather large mounds around areas of vegetation, constructing them from small sticks and other vegetable matter. One method of harvesting ants calls for planting a deep container in the midst of a mound having the top level of the container level with the surface of the mound. When the den is stirred up, the ants fall into the container. A more elaborate method, used by desert Indians, calls for the ants to be parched. A whole den of them is first shoveled onto a winnowing tray made of willow shoots. Next, the whole trayful is covered with a layer of hot coals. Then it is picked up, and the entire mass is winnowed. The hot coals kill and roast the ants as they are gradually winnowed from the coals. During this process the mound chaff is also winnowed away.

Grubs and Caterpillars

Uses: There are many varieties of grubs and caterpillars that can be utilized in soups and stews, but those with hair or fuzz on them should be avoided as some are poisonous.

Harvesting Methods: Grubs are usually located in rotten logs and stumps, but are seldom found in quantity. Caterpillars usually infest a small area and can provide protein for several meals.

Reptiles and Amphibians

The best tool for snake hunting is a digging stick (Fig. 59, p. 55). Making a special snake stick is a waste of time in a survival situation and just adds to the bulk of the gear. It is imperative that no one play with or tease a rattlesnake before killing it. After the snake is dead its head should be cut off and buried. This is especially necessary if anyone in the group has bare feet.

All reptiles and amphibians should be skinned and eviscerated before they are cooked. Snakes and lizards are the most common reptiles, but at best provide only meager sustenance for the amount of effort required to prepare them (Fig. 72). Frogs are a good source, however, when they are found in quantity in marsh areas.

It is a simple matter to shoot frogs with three-pronged arrows and a crude bow. The arrows should be long—more like spears than arrows (Fig. 73). Reed grass and cattail spikes make the best shafts, but the foreshafts or prongs should be made from hardwood. For these greasewood (*Sarcobatus*) is the finest. The bow does not need to be fancy, nor even very strong for such purposes. The distance for shooting frogs is rarely over three feet from the tip of the long arrow. The bow merely provides a speedier and more accurate propulsion than can be achieved by thrusting a spear with the arm. Therefore, a green willow bow, cut and made on the spot, will do the job (Fig. 74).

Birds

Small birds should be considered as emergency food only, for efforts to obtain them are out of proportion to the amount of nourishment they provide.

Larger birds are worthy of one's closer attention, however, and in some areas can provide substantial meat for the fire. Chucker

Fig. 72. Skinning a rattlesnake

Fig. 73. Bow and arrow used for frogs

Fig. 74. Hunting with a frog bow

partridge, quail, and sage hens are elusive targets even for a shotgun and are difficult to snare and trap. Yet, if the hunter is patient and prepared, he can capture these birds.

One can hunt sage hens successfully with arrows or throwing sticks, and can literally herd chuckers and quail along the ground in narrow canyon areas. These birds will usually not fly unless they are pressed too hard. Snares and nets can be set up in the brush in areas which they frequent, and by making periodic drives, one can literally herd them into his traps (Fig. 75).

With a throwing stick, one of the most effective yet simple weapons for survival, one can obtain more game than with any other hunting device. Any hardwood branch will do for a start. However, one should spend time constructing and practicing with a well-made stick that is balanced and beveled to fit the throwing arm (Fig. 76).

Deadfalls and snares are also very useful for hunting animals; *however, the hunting of any game animal with traps and snares is forbidden except during an extreme emergency when one is lost in the wilderness.*

Fig. 75. Bird snares

Fig. 76. Throwing stick

Deadfall Trapping

For a variety of justifiable reasons, animals often must be killed if a man is to survive in the wilds. Trapping is still one of the most humane ways to kill an animal quickly—if it is done responsibly.

Responsible trapping implies competency, and every would-be trapper should be well acquainted with the best and most humane methods of trapping animals. Any trap that simply "holds" is ranked lowest in effectiveness. Traps that kill quickly are ranked highest in effectiveness and should be considered first, if not wholly, as the method of catching an animal.

Deadfalls are the most effective. They kill instantly and usually without damage to the pelt. They are time-consuming to construct, but once in place they may be used indefinitely. With a quantity of lightweight riggers, a trapper may travel a great distance constructing the heavy parts of each trap from materials already existing in nature. Steel traps and snares are only superior if the area affords no natural materials for deadfalls.

The timing necessary to operate a deadfall trapline is quite different under survival conditions than when conventional traplines with steel traps are being used. Many times, students report to me that their traplines are too time-consuming to be effective because only six or seven good deadfalls can be set up in

Fig. 77. Paiute deadfall set

the late afternoon. Their problem is that they are not setting up deadfall lines according to a set-check pattern, which increases the number of sets each day until a good line of about one hundred traps are in operation. Set-check traplines work this way:

On the first day, construct as many triggers as you need for the entire line. This could range anywhere from fifty traps to two hundred traps, depending on your situation. Rarely can you catch enough to survive on with less than twenty traps. A hundred or more well-planned sets will provide plenty of meat and skins for survival. The size and strength of the triggers should be fairly standard, with a catch range geared to trip on a mouse as well as a fat rockchuck. Then, whether you make a set for a small or a medium-sized animal, your triggers will all be interchangeable. At least a few triggers should be larger and stronger and should be kept separate for the occasional opportunity to construct a set for larger animals like fox, coyote, or even bear. These are rare, however, and more meat can be obtained by trapping the more prolific and less cautious rodent populations.

Fig. 78. Details of Paiute deadfall

When your triggers are all made, bundle them in groups of five and pack them for easy access on the trail.

Bait should be carefully planned and cared for. Many well-planned traplines have fallen short because of insufficient bait to finish out the line in an area where bait is scarce. For most rodents, anything salty or juicy will work as bait. A dough made from ground-up grass seeds or regular flour is best. Small chunks of hard fat, cooked meat, pine nuts, ripe cactus fruits, baked edible roots, and fresh dried bundles of hay made from clover, dandelion, or other succulent plants will also work.

The challenge in some cases is to keep from nibbling away at the bait yourself, before your traps are all out! When bait is unavailable, sets can be made to trip on contact using a bright object as a lure, or as a trail set through which an animal must pass and trip the set.

Placing one hundred deadfalls initially will take approximately three days of fairly constant effort. On day one, start the line up one side of a canyon or valley, concentrating on the most plentiful types of animals in the area—which are usually small rodents. Place your sets at frequent intervals and in places frequented by the animals. Check signs carefully to be sure they are not old and try to see a

Fig. 79. Paiute deadfall trigger system

pattern of behavior in the animals' travels. For instance, in the desert, large mice and rats are abundant. They establish runs along the bases of cliffs and rocky areas, but range out into the sandy areas for food gathering. It is obvious that the rocks afford the most protection, and if food were available there, the rodents would prefer to remain near that protection. Also, in the rocks they are less cautious and more liable to enter a deadfall set. Placing trap sets nearest their natural runways will therefore be more successful than open-ground sets near where they feed at night.

Try to construct each deadfall from stones found in the immediate area. This saves a lot of hard work and also makes a less conspicuous set. Select the best possible site and make sure that the set is constructed in a permanent fashion. Any set that destroys itself upon its initial fall is not worth the effort. It must last through several successive settings. A firm base is essential and a permanent easy balance should be achieved. Rickety sets that need repeated, time-consuming balancing each time they are reset will be inefficient in the long run. When you take the time initially to shape the stone by knocking off an edge or building a firm base for it to rest on, you will save many hours later on. Fencing around deadfalls is essential and it should be well done. Natural materials from the immediate site are best.

Proceed in a definite pattern and direction in setting out the trapline. A careful accounting should be kept on where each set is located, and some signs should be left along the main trail to indicate where and how many sets are in a given general area.

The best locator sign is simply to set one rock on top of another beside the main trail, with small pebbles placed around it—one for each trap set in the immediate vicinity.

Approximately thirty traps can be set out in this fashion on the first day, in a line ranging from a mile to over five miles in length. It is best, however, to restrict the range to less than three miles, or about ten traps per mile. In areas where small animals are abundant, as many as thirty traps may be effective over and over again in a short one-mile stretch. This reduces the time needed to check them and saves energy as well.

On the morning of the second day, quickly check your first thirty traps. Reset the tripped sets, improve those needing improvement, and return to camp with your catch. Process the catch, eat, and then travel up the opposite side of the canyon or valley setting out another thirty or forty deadfalls.

Fig. 80. Figure 4 trail deadfall. This is used on game trails where brush is thick and at entrances to burrows and dens. A V-shaped row of stakes fanning away from each approach causes game to go through rather than around the logs.

Fig. 81. Details of the figure 4 trap trigger

Fig. 82. Two-stick deadfall supporting a flat stone. This is simple to construct, but is not as effective as the figure 4 trap.

Fig. 83. Another type of two-stick deadfall

Fig. 84. Bird trap. The bird hops first onto the twig and causes the stone to fall. Rattlesnakes sometimes are caught with this; therefore, one must use caution when retrieving his game.

Fig. 85. Lift pole snare

Fig. 86. Spring pole snare set on a trail.

Fig. 87. Spring pole snare with baited trigger. The snare loop is placed where it will encircle the animal's neck as it reaches for the bait.

Fig. 88. Snare with bait. A hole is drilled in the cross stick and a string threaded through it with a knot in one end, and the bait stick is lightly forced into the hole so that the knot will not slip. A small fence is set up around one side so that the animal must reach through the snare loop to get the bait.

Fig. 89. Trail set snare placed in a feed run made by water animals. The animal drags the stone anchor into the water, sinks, and drowns. A float tied to the stone reveals the position of the snare after it sinks.

Early on the third morning, check all the traps, process the catch, eat, and repeat the pattern of the second day. This time, though, set the rest of your traps in a location near areas where good catches were made during the previous two days. This insures a greater yield in the days to come without extending the area of the trapline. From that point on, the line is maintained by checking it each morning, resetting the traps that are sprung, and processing the catch. This can all be done in about three hours if the trapline is not over three miles long. Time should be taken to pull traps that do not produce and construct new sets in a new location if necessary. A few extra replacement triggers should always be carried, along with new bait. Some sets will fall on the triggers and break them.

Survival with traps is the surest way to get meat. The trapline will bring you ample food for your effort in the long run, since it is working for you while you are sleeping. That kind of economy can't be beat. The major daytime tasks of gathering plants, foods, hunting, drying meat, and doing other chores are not seriously interrupted by a trapline that is checked early in the morning.

Hunting and Stalking

Using primitive weapons to capture game is extremely different from shooting with a rifle at a deer as it runs across the canyon. In a survival situation a person must exercise all of his ability in order to get close enough to his prey for his arrows or spear to be effective (Fig. 90). But stalking deer and other large game is not difficult if one acquaints himself with a few techniques.

■ The hunter must spot the deer before it sees him.
■ He must keep downwind from the deer.
■ He must watch the deer's feeding habits until he observes a pattern. Most deer feed for about twenty seconds and then raise their heads for a look around. When their heads are down, they see nothing but the brush they are eating.
■ The hunter must slowly walk toward the animal when its head is down. As he walks he counts to ten and then stops. He must never press his luck by trying to gain a few more steps before the deer looks up, for it might catch him in the middle of a step. The hunter should make no attempt to hide; instead, he should relax in place, because the wait might be a long one. In a few seconds the deer will raise its head and survey the country but

will see only movement. When it looks in the direction of the hunter it might gaze at him for some time, but if the hunter does not even so much as bat an eyelash, the deer will soon ignore him and continue feeding.

■ The hunter should walk forward again for another ten seconds as soon as the deer drops its head, and then freeze. The hunter continues this procedure until the range is right for a good shot. Somehow a deer fails to comprehend that what appears to be an old stump gets closer each time the deer looks up.

Deer can also be ambushed at water holes during early dawn hours or in the late evening. The secret here is for one to conceal himself in a spot that does not allow the deer to sense his presence and yet does allow a clear shot. Two or more people can drive deer past hunters concealed along well-used trails.

Another technique consists of the hunter calling the animal to him. If he, for instance, learns to mimic the cry of a mouse or rabbit in pain, the hunter will be able to attract any carnivore as well as the

Fig. 90. Hunting with a primitive bow and arrow

Fig. 91. Calling game

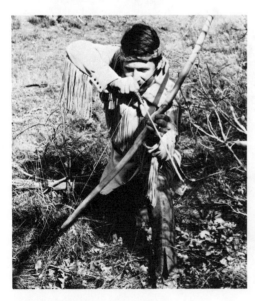

Fig. 92. Using primitive Indian technique

Fig. 93. Using a rodent skewer

animal he imitates. There are a number of ways to make good animal calls but the simplest and perhaps the finest one involves only the lips and the back of the hand. A long, drawn-out kiss on the back of a wet hand sounds (with practice) like a squaling rabbit or mouse. Short smacks sound like the call of a chipmunk or rockchuck. With a little practice a hunter can develop a number of calls using only the lips and hands (Fig. 91).

Rockchucks and ground squirrels may be easily fooled by two hunters who make an open approach to the animal's den, as one of them whistles a lively tune. When the animal dives for his hole, the hunters continue walking and the whistler, still whistling, walks on by and off into the distance. Then the other hunter quickly conceals himself in a position for a good shot and waits. The rockchuck, hearing the whistling fading in the distance,comes out for a look around; and if the concealed hunter is a good shot, he has himself a meal (Fig. 92).

Sometimes a rodent can be dragged from its den with a rodent skewer, a simple device made from a long supple willow with a small fork in one end (Fig. 93). The hunter thrusts it into the hole until he feels the animal. Then by gently twisting the stick, he catches the forked end in the animal's fur and winds it tightly. As he gently pulls and coaxes, he brings the rodent to the surface.

Ground squirrels and mice can be caught by flooding them from their holes with a diverted stream or with buckets of water. They can be killed with sticks as they emerge.

Fish

Catching fish can be difficult in outdoor survival, but if one learns a few techniques he can end up with enough for a tasty meal.

Tackle

Making fishing tackle requires some special skills in working bone and in twisting fibers for line. The fibers best suited for this are stinging nettle (*Urtica*), milkweed (*Asclepias*), dogbane (*Apocynum cannabinum*), and the bark of the haw tree (*Crataegus*). They must be selected carefully and twisted tightly (see Cordage, pp. 158). Ten feet of line on a long willow pole will serve well in most rivers and streams.

Hooks are best made of bone. The simplest is the skewer hook, which is a sliver of bone that is tied at the middle and turned parallel

Fig. 94. Skewer hook made from bone

cross hook   baited

Fig. 95. Cross hook made from bone

Fig. 96. Making hooks from bird bone   Fig. 97. Attaching hooks to line

to the line and inserted into the bait (Fig. 94). When the fish swallows the bait, the bone turns sideways and holds. Another simple device is the cross hook, the crosspiece of which is turned parallel to the main shank when the bait is applied. When the fish swallows this, the crosspiece is pulled sideways; thus, the hook is set and the fish is caught (Fig. 95).

Conventional hooks can be made of bone in the following manner:

■ A small thin-walled bone (only bird and rodent bones will do) is selected and cut into a rectangle.

■ The piece of bone is then drilled several times so that the center portion can be removed.

■ The partitions between the drill holes are removed with a stone or bone punch and the walls are smoothed with a small piece of sanding stone. The result is a rectangular ring of bone.

■ The ring is then cut in two places, and the result is two hooks which must be sharpened and then attached to a lead line (Fig. 96).

Hooks are attached to the line by a tight wrapping of fine string or fiber. The hook shank is first notched and then smeared with pitch or some other sticky substance. After the wrapping is attached, it is sealed to the hook with pitch. Hooks can be successfully tied on the line without the use of pitch, however, if the wrapping is made tight in the notches (Fig. 97).

Wishbones of small birds may also be used for hooks (Fig. 98).

Fig. 98. Hook made from wishbone of a small bird

It is extremely difficult to catch trout and other game fish in small streams with this crude equipment, but river fish such as carp, suckers, catfish, chubs, redhorse, squawfish, and whitefish are easily caught and prove to be very tasty when fried or baked.

Traps

A good fish trap will catch many more fish than a hook and line. There are several different types, all of which are good. One should build his trap according to the nature of the stream or river—his ingenuity in using natural features to aid in making the traps will determine much of his success (Figs. 99–101).

Fig. 99. Willow fish trap placed in stream riffles between pools

Fig. 100. Willow fish trap. A V-shaped barrier fence made of willows stuck in mud leading to the opening will direct migrating fish into the trap.

Spears

Many fish feed in shallow water and are easily caught with a simple spear made from a willow about 14 feet long to which is bound a set of hardwood prongs. The prongs should be bound with most of their length attached to the shaft, as this will ensure the sturdiness of the device when it is used roughly. Few fish are lost if one spears them through the sides and then pins them to the bottom by quickly pushing the spear into an upright position and forcing it into the mud (Figs. 102 and 103).

There are also several other types of spears that can be used. However, in a practical sense, none of them will serve any better than the simple one mentioned above. It may prove interesting to try them when the time warrants the effort to manufacture them (Fig. 104).

Other Water Life

A good part of wild food source lives in or near the water, and much of it is so easily caught that a person could live indefinitely from one small stream. Crayfish, mussels, helgramites, stone flies, snails,

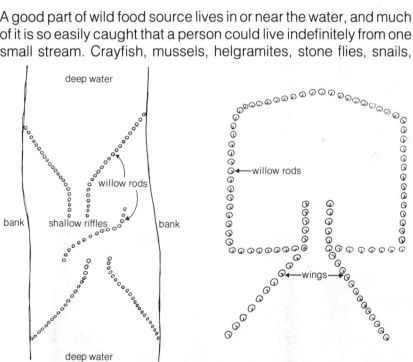

Fig. 101. Winged fish traps. These are made from willow rods driven into a stream bottom. Numerous variations of this trap are possible in most shallow streams and rivers.

Fig. 102. Making a fish spear from a willow

Fig. 103. Preparing to spear a fish

tiny minnows, and polliwogs are the most common and are found under rocks and moss or in mud along the shore. Crayfish and mussels are the most desirable and can be gathered in fairly large amounts. Mussels are sometimes found buried in the mud—a shallow trail terminating in a slight hump in the mud will betray their presence. In shallow, gravel-covered stream bottoms, they are found sticking up among the rocks. Just feel for them. Crayfish appear in the evenings and can be caught by hand or with a hook and line. One can scare them out by moving the rocks which cover them, but they must be grabbed quickly and carefully.

A willow basket trap placed in a swift-flowing stream will net crayfish, small fish, and a multitude of other water life if a proper drive is made. The survivor can do this by situating the trap so that it faces upstream and then staking it to the bottom or having another person hold it securely. Then, entering the water twenty or thirty feet upstream, he begins kicking and scuffing rocks and gravel and slowly works his way downstream toward the trap. He moves every stone and stirs the bottom vigorously. He then raises the trap, removes the catch, and places the trap in a new location. Using this technique he often catches buckets full of incredible edibles.

bone shank spear

bone

split shaft spear

Fig. 104. Some of the most effective fish spears

115

Jerky

Meat will not keep very long in warm weather; therefore, it is necessary that any surplus be dried for future use. The standard modern methods of making jerky involve brines and spices which give the meat a rich flavor. However, these processes decrease the food value and render the meat so salty that a substantial meal of nothing but jerky would make a person sick.

Meat jerked for use as a food rather than as a snack or delicacy must be prepared without brines and spices. It is merely cut into

Fig. 105. Jerky hung out to dry

Fig. 106. Cutting or unrolling jerky

116

thin strips about ¼ inch thick and dried in the sun for a couple of days. When it becomes hard and brittle, it is taken down and stored in a pit or in bags. It is then used in stews and soups or roasted lightly on the coals and eaten (Fig. 105).

Cutting meat into strips may be difficult when small chunks are involved; therefore, it is easiest if one takes a chunk and cuts through it within ¼ inch of the other side. Then by turning the knife sideways, he can cut or unroll the chunk into a long strip for drying (Fig. 106).

Small animals and birds can be dried whole. After they are skinned and eviscerated and after the back is cracked between the legs, a stick is inserted to hold the body cavity open. The animals are then laid on rocks in the sun to dry. When thoroughly dried, they are pounded until the bones are crushed. Another day in the sun will dry the marrow and ensure preservation (Figs. 107 and 108).

Pemmican

Pemmican, a mixture which surpasses the taste and nutrition of "K" rations, is made with berries which have been dried to remove the excess moisture and then pounded into a paste. Dried pounded jerky is added to this paste, and then melted suet is mixed with the

Fig. 107. Ground squirrel spread out to dry in the sun

Fig. 108. Pounding jerky

Fig. 109. Pemmican ready for eating

berries and meat. The mixture is next rolled into small balls and stored in the cleaned intestines of a large animal. Then the intestine sack is tied shut, sealed with suet, and stored in a cool, dry place. Pemmican prepared in this way will keep for several months (Fig. 109). Balls of pemmican are also safely stored in plastic bags or leather bags that are richly soaked in melted suet.

Dried Fish

Small minnows are easily dried when spread out in the sun, and it is not necessary that they be cleaned. But larger minnows of over 2½ inches long should be eviscerated and split for drying. The sun will dry small fish in one or two days after which they can be put in bags for safe keeping or placed in a storage pit for preservation.

Drying larger fish is accomplished in one of two ways. The simplest way is to split the fish down the back and hang it on a rack. Even though the bones are still intact and make eating difficult, one can get around them by pounding the dried fish into a fine meal to be used in stews. This crushes the larger bones, and the finer ones are softened by cooking.

A second method is to fillet the fish and dry the strips by hanging them on a rack in the sun. One cuts the meat from the bones after he splits the fish down the back and removes the side strips by slicing along the ribs. There is some waste if the bones are not saved, however. In a survival situation waste is not tolerable. The remaining bones can be used well if they are slightly dried and then ground into a meal to be added to stews.

All dried fish will keep a year or more if it is stored in a dry place. Eating dried fish is not always a pleasant experience at first, and there always exists the possibility of parasites. Therefore, it is best to cook the fish before it is eaten.

The advantage to pounding or grinding fish is that these processes allow the fish to dry better, thus minimizing spoilage and reducing the space taken up by bulky chunks. The fish meal has many more uses than the whole strips—it can be used in bread, soup, stew, and stuffing; mixed with cooked seed grains for a wholesome cereal; and moistened, made into fish patties, and fried.

7

Fig. 110. Straightening an arrow shaft

SPECIAL SKILLS

In an outdoor survival situation, man can use only the natural elements around him for constructing tools; therefore, he must know how to use nature effectively (Fig. 110). The following explanations of a few of the more important methods of making and using primitive tools will be helpful, but one must realize that common sense is the key and that many other methods will also work.

The skills discussed here are presented exactly as the author has used them while living off the land. They appear in this order: working stone, working bone, constructing bows and arrows, constructing atlatls and spears, making cordage, preparing sinew, weaving sandals and baskets, making rawhide, and tanning skins.

Working Stone

Ancient man's survival depended in great measure upon his ability to utilize and modify his immediate surroundings. To accomplish the tasks of cutting, digging, scraping, chopping, and building, he developed a remarkable array of tools made of stone. The skills required to produce such workable tools are more complex than one might imagine and show evidence of a high degree of inventiveness and manual dexterity. The amount of work that can be done with these tools is indeed remarkable.

A person thrown into a primitive survival situation would quickly find his existence greatly impaired without the aid of so simple a tool as a pocketknife. It would seem that he could never survive without a knife to cut poles for building shelters, to cut shafts for a spear or bow, or to fashion the myriad items essential for survival. The construction of almost everything requires the direct or indirect use of a cutting or chopping edge which is itself fashioned with other tools made with cutting and chopping tools (Figs. 111 and 112).

The more common primitive methods of working stone which are discussed here I carefully researched and repeatedly tested until I achieved mastery of them.

The processes of shaping stone can be divided into four major areas: (1) percussion flaking, (2) pressure flaking, (3) pecking or crumbling, and (4) abrading. Other recognized processes such as incising and piercing are minor and can be included as simple variations of the abrading process under special conditions. They are used exclusively to shape very soft rocks such as soapstone.

Percussion Flaking

Percussion flaking, a highly technical art demanding precise skill and forethought, consists of three methods: (1) direct percussion with a hammerstone, (2) indirect percussion with a hammerstone and a punch, and (3) direct or indirect percussion with the stone resting on another larger stone (anvil). All three methods can be used in the production of a single piece of work.

Direct percussion, also called direct freehand percussion, can be used for shaping large pieces of rock into blanks from which specialized tools can be fashioned. In practice, the stone to be shaped is held in the left hand and fractured with blows from a hammerstone or horn baton held in the right hand. Simple axes and choppers can be made in this manner from common rhyolite or quartzite cobbles. The blows of the hammerstone should fall directly onto the edge of the core, especially if it is a rather thin one. This is necessary for working chert, coarse agate, dull jasper, or any other nonglassy stone. Holding the blank at an angle while striking off chips is often necessary for removing rough spots and trimming edges. For instance, obsidian and other similar glassy rocks cannot be chipped successfully if they are struck directly on the edge of the core. The core must be struck at an angle if crumbling edges and unwanted hinge fractures are to be avoided (Fig. 113).

Fig. 111. Chopping tools

Fig. 112. Cutting tools

Fig. 113. Striking flakes. (a) Striking directly into hard shale or cobble stone; (b) Striking glassy rock (obsidian or jasper) at an angle with the hammerstone; (c) Striking flakes from glassy stones incorrectly; (d) Striking flakes by indirect percussion.

Fig. 114. Striking the core with a horn baton

Fig. 115. Blade struck from the core

When cutting blades or other specialized tools are needed, a striking platform must be constructed on the core. This is done by merely breaking a rock in half, leaving two cores, each with one flat surface. Striking blades from the core is then relatively easy. If the stroke carries all the way through the core, good blades will be produced consistently. If the core is worked around with even strokes, a number of razor-sharp blades can be made before the core is exhausted (Figs. 114 and 115).

If a blank has a difficult knob or thick edge in such a place as to make direct percussion impractical, it can be worked down indirectly with the aid of a punch made from deer antler or other antler of similar density. This process requires the assistance of a second person. The blank is held in the left hand, which is protected with a leather pad, and the punch is placed against the edge of the blank and steadied with the other hand. The assistant then strikes the punch sharply with a hammerstone. In this way the force is applied to the exact spot intended.

Percussion flaking with the blank resting on another stone (anvil) works but is rarely necessary except for removing troublesome knobs and for striking off larger flakes to thin down a thick blank. For this it is best to use the indirect percussion method with the blank resting on a padded anvil.

A variation of the indirect percussion method calls for the blank to be placed between the knees with the edge to be flaked facing up. A person can then use the punch and hammerstone without the aid of an assistant. There is no danger that the chips will cut the knees if the blank is placed in the fold of a thick piece of leather. Variations of this sort are numerous among modern flintworkers and were probably popular in aboriginal times. The use of one method and not another is merely a matter of preference. Basically, the simple use of only the hammerstone or antler baton in shaping tools is the most practical form of percussion flaking.

Pressure Flaking

The more delicate job of finishing a blank into a specialized implement requires the simplest of tools but a complex nervous system. A nervous Indian probably spent more time bandaging his cuts than making arrowheads. A piece of antler and a leather pad are all that is needed for producing the finest knives and arrowpoints (Fig. 116). A blank or blade produced by percussion flaking or a simple chip of flint or obsidian is held in the palm of the left hand with the fingers gripping it firmly. A leather pad protects the hand from being cut. The hand is braced against the left knee, and small chips are pressed off of the blank with the antler flaker. The tip of the antler is placed on the edge of the flint and pressure is applied inward and downward against it. At the same time, a slight twist is applied to the antler, causing the chip to come off of the underside of the blank. Considerable skill is required for superior work, but one can turn out good serviceable tools in a short time with only a little practice (Fig. 117).

A further consideration of the minute technicalities of pressure flaking reveals that there is considerably more to it than just the basics previously described.

■ The stone must be held slightly forward on the heel of the hand when the stone is gripped in one hand and braced against the knee, so that the pressure from the fingers will tip the edge up. This allows the flaker tip to force the chip off the bottom side of the blank. Failure to do this can result in the quick reduction of the number of fingers on the hand of even the most skilled Stone Age artisan.

■ The power of the wrist is not sufficient for flaking larger pieces of stone; hence the force applied with the tip of the flaker must come from the weight of the body. The push should be fairly hard but not sudden. The best results are achieved by just leaning the body into the tip of the flaker with a steady even pressure. Sudden hard lunges cause loss of control and often result in bad cuts.

Fig. 116. Pressure flaking with a horn and a pad

- The tip of the flaker is not sharpened to a fine point but is given a blunt chisel shape. This allows it to grip the blank firmly.
- The force is applied in the direction in which the flake should run. The objective is to make the flake run across the bottom face of the blank. If the tool is pushed downward at a 90° angle, the flake will be short and stubby.
- The flake comes off more readily if the force of the flaker, as it is applied against the edge of the blank, is accompanied by a slight twist.

The method of pressure flaking described above is the most widely used. One variation of it uses a stone anvil as a rest and is similar to indirect rest percussion. The only difference is that instead of the flakes being struck off they are pressed off with the punch. Here again individual preference is the rule. At any rate, all of the possible methods used for percussion and pressure flaking can be combined and modified to accomplish the task of flaking stone into useful tools.

Antler and leather are the tools used for pressure flaking, but only the student trained under civilized exactness would fail to improvise suitable substitutes. The archaic craftsman caught without his chipping kit would replace the leather with a pad of sagebrush bark, a flat piece of tree bark, or some green moss. In place of the antler, he would use a bone or tooth fragment set in a wooden handle. He might even use a hardwood stick or a sliver of rock, though these do not work as well. The ability to improvise a variety of techniques in working stone cannot be underestimated.

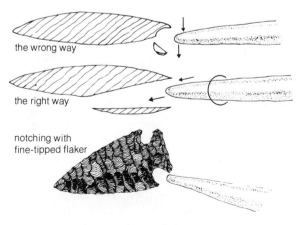

the wrong way

the right way

notching with
fine-tipped flaker

Fig. 117. Details of pressure flaking

Pecking or Crumbling

Shaping stones by crumbling them requires relatively little brain-power, but a lot of perseverance and resignation to monotony. A caveman working stone probably often reached the nervous-breakdown point when he shattered his newly finished axehead with that final perfectionist's tap. I can almost hear the canyons ringing with whatever verbal abuses entered his primeval mind.

The king of stone working implements, the hammerstone, is all that is needed for this process. With it, and infinite patience, have been shaped colossal stelae and monumental blocks of solid stone for temples. However, primitive man, for the most part, was content to use the simple hammerstone for making axes, club-heads, mortars and pestles, metates and manos, and various other necessary items (Fig. 118). Hammerstones are best made from quartzite cobbles and can have a variety of shapes and sizes. To use them one has only to start pecking away at another rock, preferably one that is slightly softer than the hammerstone. The strokes should be even and rapid, and not too hard, and they should be kept up until the surface of the stone being shaped starts to crumble away into a fine dust. The rock being shaped should

Fig. 118. Using the hammerstone

Fig. 119. Sharpening an axehead

never rest on a solid surface as it will crack under the blows of the hammerstone. It should be held loosely in the hand. In this way the tool slowly takes shape. The crumbling process is speeded up if water is applied to the crumbling surface. Axes are generally roughly shaped by percussion flaking with the hammerstone before they are submitted to the crumbling process. A good axehead can be turned out in about one hour, and another hour of grinding and polishing will give it the touch of beauty found in the finest Southwestern stonework (Fig. 119).

One can easily haft an axe by heating a slender willow, wrapping it twice around the axehead, and securing it in place by wrapping it with willow shoots or cord. This type of axe handle will hold tightly and withstand a good deal of abuse (Figs. 120–121). This method of hafting axes is unequaled for efficiency and ease of handling.

Abrading

Grinding, cutting, sawing, drilling, scraping, whetting, rasping, and polishing are all part of the abrading process. The use of abrasion is important in shaping and finishing stones used in food

Fig. 120. Wrapping the handle on

Fig. 121. Completed hafting of the axehead

preparation, because the smoothing of grinding implements reduces much of the grit content in foodstuffs. The cutting edges of implements made of granular stones such as basalt and slate can be honed to perfection by abrasion.

Grinding and whetting stone simply requires another stone upon which the implement is rubbed. The best abrading stones are sandstone and other granular rocks that contain hard pieces of silica. Sand poured on the surface of the abrading stone is used as an effective abrasive. The use of water to speed up the process is effective. Even the hardest agates can be ground and polished if they are rubbed against a simple abrasive. Like the crumbling process, abrasion takes time and patience. Except for honing cutting edges and smoothing food-grinding implements, grinding and polishing stone are largely used for giving a finished look to tools that are already serviceable.

Cutting or sawing stone is accomplished not with a tooth-edged stone saw but by simple abrasion with thin slabs of an abrasive stone. Jade and other tough materials are beautifully carved and grooved with simple slab saws and the use of sand and water as abrasive agents.

Drilling stone is accomplished in a number of ways, but the most common method consists of a pump drill with a stone bit. The bit is necessarily made of very hard material, jasper and agate being the finest. With a good pump drill it is a simple matter to drill slate, chert, basalt, rhyolite, or any other soft stone. Even hard stone can in time be penetrated if fine quartz sand is used as an abrasive. Water added to the work in most forms of drilling speeds up the process but one must replenish it repeatedly in addition to keeping the hole clean if grit is to be kept from forming a thick paste and choking up the drill (Fig. 123).

Another drill consists of a simple stick drill with a stone bit. This device is twirled between the hands. The simplest drill is merely a bit grasped in the fingers and twisted back and forth into the material being drilled.

Stone bits are usually necessary for getting the hole started. But after a shallow hole is formed in the stone, a bone or hardwood bit can be substituted, with sand serving as an abrasive. Bone and wood bits grip the grains of sand, causing them to cut rapidly into the stone. Water cannot be used with a wooden drill bit as it causes the wood to swell and bind.

Stone Versus Steel

The utility of primitive stone tools compared to the utility of modern metal tools leaves little doubt as to which is superior. At the same time, however, stone cannot be regarded as totally inferior. For instance, flint arrowpoints are entirely equal to steel heads in their penetrating power; stone axeheads, though somewhat slower, will cut down a tree with as much sureness as the finest steel axe; a stone drill bit will make as neat a hole as a high-carbon steel bit; and a flint knife will skin a deer and cut it up as well as a modern butcher knife.

Thus, it seems reasonable to a few artisans dedicated to primitive skills that mastery of the techniques of the Stone Age is imperative to true outdoor survival. A survivor will not get very far if he uses methods that are not authentic, if, for instance, he believes that Indians made arrowheads with fire and a wet straw. But he can be master of almost any situation if he applies actual techniques.

Fig. 123. Using the pump drill

Fig. 122. Chopping a willow with the axe

Working Bone

Cutting and carving bones into useful implements presents some special problems when one is working with stone tools only. But a few tips on handling bone-working implements will greatly reduce the time and sweat required to make a simple bone tool.

■ For splitting bones, the tool of value is a graver, which one can make easily by flaking a small sharp nipple on the edge of a piece of hard stone, preferably agate or jasper. It is used to scratch a light groove down the length of a bone. The cut is then deepened with the application of rapid strokes made with the graver tip, the groove serving as a guide channel. This process is repeated on the opposite side of the bone. Next, the bone is placed on a stone and tapped with a small rock. The tapping is repeated all along the edges of the grooves until the bone splits (Figs. 124–126).

■ For notching bones, a stoneflake is needed. Sometimes one needs a bone tool with notches so that he can tie on strings or cut jagged edges, and these are easily carved with a stone flake.

■ For sharpening and honing bones, a sanding stone is required (Fig. 127). The bone is rubbed back and forth on a rough stone surface and finished on a finer sanding stone. Small pieces of bone can be ground between two sanding surfaces. As the two stones are rubbed back and forth, the bone between them is ground rapidly.

■ For drilling bones, the processes are exactly the same as those described for drilling stone (p. 130).

Fig. 124. Scratching a groove with the graver

Fig. 125. Tapping a grooved bone with a small rock

Fig. 126. Split bone and finished awl made from a split bone

Fig. 127. Sharpening a bone awl with a sanding stone

133

Fig. 128. Taking the shot

Fig. 129. Determining the length of the bow

Constructing Bows and Arrows

An archer under primitive conditions is somewhat different from the modern bowman with his laminated finery. His equipment even at best is vastly inferior, hence his success in hunting depends more on patience, practice, good luck, and a keen stalking ability that allows him close shots. But the value of the primitive bow and arrow must never be underestimated, as they are an important aid in filling the stewpot. The perfect shot quite often presents itself in the wilderness, and it is the wise hunter who has something to take the shot with (Fig. 128).

Bows

The finest woods for making bows include mountain mahogany (*Cercocarpus*), ash (*Fraxinus*), serviceberry (*Amelanchier*), and chokecherry (*Prunus*). A sapling burned by a brushfire is excellent bow wood. Many trees uprooted by wind also have well-seasoned branches. But a dead tree with its roots still in the ground may be too brittle or too weathersplit for use, unless it has been killed by fire.

Since preseasoned wood is rare in the wilderness, greenwood usually has to fill the need, and if carefully cured it is superior to other woods. A straight stave that is free from knots and small branches should be selected, and the stave should be carefully cut clear through, not broken off. It is the wise survivor who selects two or three staves to work with—an extra bow stuck in the belt is good insurance. The bow described here is a "quickie bow" using the style of the Bushmen. Flat Indian bows are better, but take more time in a survival situation.

The measurements of a bow will vary with the available supply, but too often staves are selected that are too large in diameter. The best diameter is from one to two inches at the handgrip. This must be determined *before* the bark is removed.

The length should be approximately 44 inches, but this will vary with each person. A good method of determining length is for one to hold the stave on a horizontal plane extending from the left shoulder to the tip of the fingers of the extended right arm (Fig. 129).

Once the staves are selected and measured, the bark should be scraped off and left overnight in a cool but dry place. The staves

Fig. 130. Determining the natural bend of the bow

Fig. 131. Scraping the bow staff

must not be exposed to sunlight for the first six hours after the bark is removed.

The process of shaping a bow requires more than skill; it demands sensitivity and patience as well. Every stave, no matter how straight, has a natural bend to it which one can determine by placing the butt end on the ground and holding the stave vertical with his left hand in the middle where the handgrip will be. He then grasps the tip of the stave with his right hand and pulls it toward him lightly. The stave will turn in his left hand and settle into its natural bend. The side of the stave facing away from him then becomes the back of the bow (Fig. 130).

Only after the bend is determined should the actual shaping of the bow commence. Holding the stave with the butt, or larger, end pointing down, one can determine the exact location of the center of the handgrip and mark it with a scratch. Next he trims the upper half of the bow to the exact dimensions he desires, completing the top before starting the lower half. There is good reason for this which will become apparent if one does not comply with the directions.

Trimming the bow stave to its final dimensions should be done by sight alone. Each half is gracefully tapered from the center to the end in an even plane which results in a pointed tip. The circumference should be kept round from the handgrip to the tips. If the diameter of the bow is somewhat larger than expected, the belly of the bow can be flattened, but only to the degree that the bow becomes more flexible along its entire length.

One should never draw the bow during its construction to test it. Testing can be done by *slightly* bending the bow at intervals and judging its strength or stiffness by sight and weight. A good bow will look good and will be graceful and light.

The actual trimming and shaping process should *not* be done by whittling. Rather the excess wood should be scraped off in long even strokes from the handgrip to the tips (Fig. 131). A piece of flint, agate, jasper, or obsidian does the best job, but broken glass and steel knife blades are also effective. However, if one uses a knife blade he feels strongly tempted to speed up the process by whittling with it, and this ruins a bow stave. Most staves cut in the wilderness catch the blade and guide the cut in a spiral around them, thus causing the carver to remove too much wood in a small area and to make an uneven taper.

Holding a stone blade with sharp edges at a right angle to the stave, one can shave off thin strips of wood in much the same manner as when he uses a plane (Fig. 132). This tool is sometimes called a planar scraper or a flake blade (Fig. 133).

When the bow is finished it should be stored away for a day or two to cure. One can speed up the curing process, however, by holding the bow over hot coals or standing it by the fire.

When the bow is dry it should be greased with all of the animal fat it can absorb. The survivor should then heat the bow and rub it until his arm aches. Fat can be obtained from any animal, even a mouse. If fat is not available, fish oil can be obtained from several chopped and boiled fish. The oil is skimmed off the water and rubbed on the bow. If oil is not available, the bow can be used as it is.

I was once severely criticized during a survival expedition by my companions and made to walk downwind from them for braving the stench of an old deer carcass to obtain some sinew and a chunk of rancid fat. However, they envied my efforts several days later when I completed a fine serviceberry wood bow and used the rancid fat and sinew to finish it off. We were miles away from the deer carcass by then and they gratefully shared my treasure for their own bows. After that we all smelled the same.

After his bow is cured and greased, the survivor can give it a final shaping by recurving the tips. This involves heating the tip of the bow over hot coals and then bending it over a smooth, round stone, holding it in position until it cools (Fig. 134).

Fig. 132. Planning the bow with a flint chip

Fig. 133. Planar scrapers and flake blades

Fig. 134. Recurving the bow tips

Fig. 135. Roughening the bow tips   Fig. 136. Smearing pitch on the bow tip

Fig. 137. Wrapping sinew on the bow tip

The tips can be notched to receive or left smooth. Smooth tips prevent splitting, but the tips should be scratched with a flint chip to roughen the surface, then smeared with hot, boiled pine pitch, and wrapped with sinew from the tip down, about three inches (Figs. 135–137). This provides a no-slip surface to tie the bowstring to and prevents the tips of the bow from splitting.

The bow is then strung when the string is tied permanently to one end, wrapped around the other end two or three times, and secured with two half hitches (Fig. 138).

The bow is now complete. It should be shot with the stave held on the same plane in which it originally grew in the bush—the butt end pointing down and the tip up. It should be kept unstrung when not in use and greased regularly (Fig. 139).

In a survival situation, a quickie bow, such as this, will do the job admirably for a patient and skilled hunter. The least amount of time in which it can be made is two days, if all the materials are available. Primitive man usually spent a great deal more time and consequently produced more lasting equipment, but it was not necessarily more effective.

The bow just described is capable of killing large game as well as rabbits, squirrels, and birds. But it is only as effective as its maker and user.

Fig. 138. Stringing the bow

Fig. 139. Finished bow

Bowstrings

The strongest bowstrings are made from sinew (see Preparing Sinew, p. 159), but nettle, milkweed, and some barks are usable substitutes, though inferior. The string should be at least twelve inches longer than the bow.

Sinew strands are twisted together for bowstring in this manner: two strands of sinew are held in the left hand and pinched together between the thumb and second joint of the forefinger; then the strand that is farthest from the body is twisted clockwise with the right hand and then folded back over the first one in the same manner. This process is continued until the required length is achieved. Splicing new length to the cord is done by carefully laying the new cord alongside the last inch of the old cord strand and twisting the two together. If the ends are carefully tapered for splicing with a sharp-edged tool, the diameter of the cord will not be increased (Figs. 140–144).

A sinew string is finished by stretching it between two points and rubbing saliva into it until all the rough spots are smoothed down. It must then dry in this position.

Fig. 140. Proper position for holding sinew Fig. 141. Twisting counter-clockwise

Fig. 142. Folding the twisted strand over the other strand

Fig. 143. Adding new strands to the cord Fig. 144. Twisting in the new strands

Fig. 145. Preparing reeds for arrowshafts

Fig. 146. Cutting the tip end below the joint

Arrows

Several different kinds of serviceable arrow shafts can be constructed. Since feathers are at a premium in a wilderness situation, arrows are often made without them. And when feathers are available, glue for fletching them is sometimes not. Because of these limitations, one can see that methods of arrow production used under primitive conditions are vastly different from those used in ordinary circumstances. As a result the end products differ in many ways.

Arrows without fletchings are made from light woods and reeds. The common river reed (*Phragmites communis*) is best for such arrows. But willow (*Salix*) and a variety of light pithy woods can be used when reeds are not available (Fig. 145).

Reeds suitable for arrows are cut when dry. The length of each shaft should be about 24 inches, and the cuts should be made 1/2 inch above a joint on what will be the nock end and 3 or 4 inches below a joint on what will be the tip end (Figs. 146 and 148). This allows a strong place for the nock to be cut and leaves a hollow tube at the other end to receive a foreshaft. A reed shaft is straightened by rubbing grease (if available) on its joints and holding it over hot coals or on a hot rock until it is heated and then lightly bending it until it is straight, or as straight as one can make it (Fig. 147). It must be held in this position until it is cool. Reed stems are difficult to straighten between the joints, and one must be careful

Fig. 147. Straightening the reed shaft

not to break them during the straightening process. Pitch is applied and sinew is wrapped around the tip end of the shaft to keep it from splitting. The nock is cut at the tip and wrapped with sinew for added strength (Fig. 148).

Foreshafts are cut from any heavy hardwood tree or brush in 6- to 8-inch lengths. One end is sharpened to a point and hardened in a fire, and the other end is blunted and inserted into the hollow end of the reed stem. The arrow is then complete (Fig. 149).

These flimsy arrows are best used with a lightweight bow and prove effective for flock shooting and small game. A dozen or more of them can be made in one evening around the fire. They may last for only a few shots, but the simplicity and speed with which they are constructed makes them important and effective arrows. These same reed shafts can be made more accurate and deadly by the addition of stone points and fletchings (Fig. 150).

Native woods best suited for sturdy hunting arrows are chokecherry (*Prunus*), serviceberry (*Amelanchier*), rose (*Rosa*), currant

Fig. 148. Wrapping the nock end

Fig. 149. Completed arrow

(*Ribes*), and willow (*Salix*). The shafts are selected from young shoots found in shaded areas where they must grow tall and straight to reach the sunlight. After they are cut, they must be dried in the sun for one day. The bark is then peeled and the still green shafts are cut into lengths several inches longer than the standard size for the finished arrows. Next, they are sorted according to size and weight, tied into bundles of five or six, and left to dry slowly in the shade for two days. One can speed up the drying process by placing the shafts in the sunlight or by holding them over hot coals, but the danger of splitting is increased when quick drying is used. However, effective arrow shafts can be turned out within a few hours after they are cut if they are dried with heat. It is very important that the shafts be completely dry before they are made into arrows. If one makes arrows in groups of five, completing each step with all five arrows before going on, much time is saved and the arrows are better matched for more accurate shooting.

Straightening wood shafts is simple and is done in the same manner as that described for straightening reed shafts. All one has to do is heat the crooked part and work it over his knee or with his

Fig. 150. Reed arrows with stone-tipped foreshafts

fingers. An arrow wrench, which is a flat bone with a hole drilled in it, is also effective for prying out crooks (Fig. 151).

But one can get the job done much faster by gripping the shaft with his teeth just below the crook and then wrenching it straight with his hands (Fig. 152).

When the shafts are completely straight and dry, they are scraped down and smoothed with a chip of stone or broken glass (Fig. 153). Scraped lengthwise, the shafts become round and even. If a stone tip is to be used, the nock for the bowstring should be at the large end of the shaft. If the point is going to be simply sharpened and hardened in the fire, the nock should be made in the small end. Nocking the shaft for the bowstring is done by sawing the shaft with a sharp chip of stone (Fig. 154). The nock should be U-shaped and about 1/4 inch deep.

Fletching an arrow by hand is not difficult if one uses glue. The feathers are bound in place until the glue dries and then the ends of the feathers are secured with sinew. Animal glue is made by boiling down skins, hooves, or fish skins. Some plants contain a sticky sap which is also effective. But pine pitch and plant sap are not good fletching materials.

Fig. 151. Prying out crooks with an arrow wrench

Fig. 152. Straightening an arrow shaft

Fig. 153. Smoothing the arrow shaft

Fig. 154. Nocking the shaft with a stone chip

Since animal glue is difficult to make, fletching without glue often becomes necessary in the wilderness. To accomplish this, one selects long feathers from the same bird wing or from the same side of the bird's tail. He then splits them down the center of the quill with a fine chip of obsidian or other sharp stone. Next he sits on the ground and holds one end of the feather on a smooth rock with his big toe, and stretching the feather taut with his left hand, he scrapes away the excess spine with a sharp stone chip (Fig. 155). A little practice will enable him to prepare feathers with professional accuracy.

All of the feathers are then cut to the same length, 4 to 6 inches, and one inch of the web is stripped off at the base. They are attached to the shaft in the following manner:

- First, one measures the point on the shaft that the web of the feather will reach when fully fletched.
- Then he measures up the shaft toward the *nock* about one inch—the distance from the tip of the stripped quill to the beginning of the web.
- He places one feather on the shaft upside down and inverts it so that the tip of its base is even with the one-inch mark on the shaft.
- He binds the stripped end of the feather to the shaft in this position, using only one or two wraps of sinew.
- He then places the other two feathers in the same position as the first feather and binds all of them down tightly with sinew, again using only one or two wrappings.
- He lifts each feather, bending the quill at the point where the web starts, and lays it flat against the shaft. The tips on the top end of the feathers he does not strip but lightly ruffles them back and dampens them with his fingers to hold them out of the way.
- He wraps sinew over the ends of the feathers, just below the nock, leaving enough feather tip sticking out for him to grasp with his fingers.
- Grasping each tip with his fingers or with an improvised pair of pinchers, he pulls them tight, thus flattening the quill against the shaft and stiffening the vane.
- Finally, he wraps on additional sinew to secure the feathers tightly, allows the sinew to dry, and trims off the excess with a stone chip (Figs. 156–162).

A simpler method of fletching calls for a small amount of hot pine pitch to be smeared on the shaft where the ends of the

Fig. 155. Scraping away the excess spine   Fig. 156. Measuring the web position

Fig. 157. Binding feathers to the shaft in the inverted position

151

feathers will be located and also just below the nock where the tip ends of the feathers will be bound. The pitch keeps the fletchings from pulling loose. The feathers are then pressed firmly into the warm pitch and wrapped with sinew. Next, the tip ends of the fletching are bound down and pulled to flatten the quill against the shaft (Figs. 161 and 162).

When one begins the process of attaching points, he discovers that filing a notch to receive a stone or bone point is hard work without a steel knife. It is much easier to break out a notch by using this old trick:

■ A notch is cut on each side of the shaft at the point where the shaft length has been determined. This should present no

Fig. 158. Bending and laying feathers flat against the shaft

Fig. 159. Wrapping the ends of the feathers

Fig. 160. Trimming the excess feathers   Fig. 161. Pressing the feathers into the pitch

Fig. 162. Both methods of fletching

problem because the shaft was previously cut several inches longer than was necessary.

■ Another notch is cut on each side of the shaft between the first two notches 1/4 inch above them.

■ The excess shaft then breaks off when submitted to gentle pressure and bending, and a deep notch is left in the end which receives the head (Fig. 163).

Before fitting the point to the shaft, one should smooth and sand the notch to fit the contour of the point. The point is then inserted in the notch, wrapped with sinew, and, if possible, glued with pitch. When the sinew is dry, the arrow is complete and ready for use (Fig. 164).

Constructing Atlatls and Spears

A simple but effective weapon for large game is the atlatl. This device predates the bow and arrow and was used anciently to hunt large game. The Australian aborigines, the Eskimos, and some Mexican Indians still use it.

The atlatl is a stick used to throw a light spear or dart with greater force and distance than is possible with just the arm. It acts as an extension to the arm, thus giving greater power to the thrower. The atlatl is about 2 feet long, 2 inches wide, and 1/2 inch thick. A prong is carved at one end to fit into the hollow butt of the spear, and 2 loops are tied at the other end through which the fingers of the thrower pass (Fig. 165).

The spear or dart is about 5 or 6 feet long with a foreshaft of hardwood about 6 inches long, tipped with a stone point. The butt end is hollowed to receive the prong of the atlatl, and two feathers are tied to the sides near the butt end to help balance the spear in flight. The spear shaft may be made of reed grass or any straight shoot. A young straight juniper shoot is excellent but rarely found. Pine saplings growing in dense thickets are sometimes straight and slender, but any shaft can be straightened by heating and bending.

A hole is drilled in the tip end to receive the foreshaft, and cord is wrapped around the drilled end to keep it from splitting on impact. The feathering of the shaft need not be elaborate; two feathers tied securely with sinew at both ends at the middle will do. The finished spear should be slender and not too heavy or cumbersome (Fig. 166).

Fig. 163. Breaking out a notch

Fig. 164. Stone-tipped arrows

Fig. 165. Atlatl—throwing board and details of the spear foreshaft

Included here are a few suggestions which will aid the survivor as he constructs the atlatl and spear:

■ A natural bump or twig may be utilized for the prong on the atlatl.
■ The wood is carved and shaped with stone tools in the same manner as that described for making arrows.
■ Drilling a foreshaft socket is done best with a stone or bone drill set in the ground or held between the feet. The shaft is then twirled on it by being spun between the palms of the hands (Fig. 167).

Using the atlatl with skill demands much practice, and for this blunt spears without foreshafts should be used. They are also good for hunting small game. A snapping powerful throw is not necessary for using the spear. Rather it should be thrown over-handed with an even sweeping motion straight at the target, not lobbed over to it. When the butt end of the spear tends to dip down, thus spoiling its flight, it is a sign that the thrower is flipping it too hard or that the spear is too heavy (Figs. 168 and 169).

Fig. 166. Finished spear

Fig. 167. Drilling a shaft by spinning it

Fig. 168. Correct position for throwing the spear or dart

Fig. 169. Throwing the spear or dart

157

Making Cordage

Strange as it may seem, a piece of string can become the most important item in a survival situation, for the construction of nearly everything requires this simple item. Equally surprising is the simplicity with which it can be manufactured in nature. Anything from sewing thread to rope can be made from a number of common wayside plants.

Materials

Listed here are the common fibers which serve best for particular types of cordage:

■ Stinging Nettle, *Urtica* (Colorplate 20, p. 204). The stalks of this plant contain a fiber that is very strong. When the stalks are dry, one pounds them to remove the woody parts and cleans the fiber by hand. It can be used to make such things as thread, fishline, string, yarn, snares, nets, ropes, cloth, bowstrings, sandals, blankets, and woven sacks.

■ Milkweed, *Asclepias* (Colorplate 16, p. 200). The stalks of this plant contain a silky fiber that can be used when the plant is green or dry. Best when harvested dry, it is processed in the same way as nettle and can serve for the same purposes.

■ Dogbane, *Apocynum cannabinum* (Colorplate 9, p. 193). This plant is perhaps the best fiber plant found in the West. The stalks contain a fine, soft, silky fiber that is easily worked. It is processed and used the same as are nettle and milkweed.

■ Haw, Hawthorn, or Thornapple, *Crataegus*. The inner white bark of this plant makes good cordage. Though it cannot be used for as many different products as the fiber plants just listed, it can be stripped and twisted into string and rope and will serve in a pinch for fishline, snares, and sandals. The bark is strongest when wet and becomes a little stiff when dry. Other trees which have similar bark that is good for cordage are willow, elm, spruce (roots), rose, and snowberry.

■ Sagebrush, *Artemisia tridentata* (Colorplate 26, p. 210). This plant has a dry bark which can be stripped from the trunks and twisted into cordage. Though this bark is not strong, it has a wide variety of uses. It can be made into coarse woven bags and blankets and is the principal cordage for making sandals. The rope made from it is not very strong but will serve for tying things together and for holding timbers in position for shelters. It may also be pounded and used for tinder. Other plants that have similar bark are juniper trees (*Juniperus*) and cliffrose (*Cowania*). The barks of all these plants can be gathered in large quantities and used for bedding and thatching material.

Twisting

After one has collected his materials, he is ready for the more involved part of making cordage. Listed here are the various steps involved in twisting fibers by hand—they are essentially the same steps as those discussed in the section on making bowstring (p. 142).

- Two strips of fiber are selected and held in the left hand between the thumb and forefinger.
- The fiber farthest from the body is grasped in the fingers of the right hand and twisted clockwise.
- The twisted strand is then laid counterclockwise over the other strand and becomes the one closest to the body.
- The second strand (now farthest from the body) is twisted and laid over the first strand in the same manner. This is continued until the ends of the strands are reached.
- Other lengths of fiber are spliced on at this point. One does this by twisting the last two inches of the ends onto the new fibers and continuing the process of twisting and folding. It is best to alternate the lengths of the strands so that both splices do not appear at the same place in the finished string.

When short lengths of string are needed for tying something or sewing a few switches, there is a quick way to produce them. The person simply holds one end of a long strand in his left hand and rolls it in one direction on his thigh with his right hand. When it is rolled tight, he grasps one end in each hand and places the middle in his teeth. Then he puts the two ends together and holds them tightly. Next, he drops the end that is in his teeth and the string twines together automatically from the tension produced when it was twisted and rolled on the thigh. This results in a two-ply cord which is half the length of the original strand.

Preparing Sinew

The long tendons from the legs of animals and the longer ones from their backs can be prepared and fashioned into cordage that is unequaled in strength. The best bowstrings are made from sinew (see Bowstrings, p. 142). The simple strands also serve to haft arrowpoints and other tools to their wooden shafts. They are wrapped on while wet and do not need to be tied since the sinew is sticky enough to produce its own glue.

When the tendons are taken from the animal, they should be cleaned and placed in the sun until they are completely hard and dry and then placed on a smooth rock and pounded with another rock until they are soft, fluffy, and white. The sinew will then strip apart into fine threads. It can be used dry for sewing thread, twisted into cords, or moistened for wrapping and hafting stone implements (Fig. 170).

Weaving Clothes and Other Items

Like anything else that is worthwhile, weaving takes time. But a number of useful items can be made with the simple plain weave, an over-and-under technique. Cattail and bulrush stems produce good mats for floor coverings, beds, and shelter covers.

The twining method is used for making blankets, bags, sandals, fish traps, and some baskets. The foundation strands are called the warp and the interwoven strands are called the weft. There are two weft strands in twining, one going over the warp and the other under it, and they are crossed between each warp.

Most baskets used for water bottles and for carrying and harvesting seeds are made with the coiled technique. A basket is built up from the base with a growing spiral coil consisting of two small withes of willow and a bundle of fibrous material, usually grass or bark. Each coil is then stitched to the one below with a thin splint of cambium layer squaw bush or willow. The splint is passed through the coil with the aid of a bone awl (Fig. 171).

There are some items and processes one should be aware of as he weaves which will make his work more efficient and save him time.

■ Grasses and reeds selected for weaving should be dry and not green.

■ The dried material should be soaked in water just before it is used and kept pliable during the weaving process.

■ Willow weaving materials should be cut when green, split twice to the cambium layer, left to dry, and soaked in water just before they are used.

160

Fig. 170. Prepared sinew

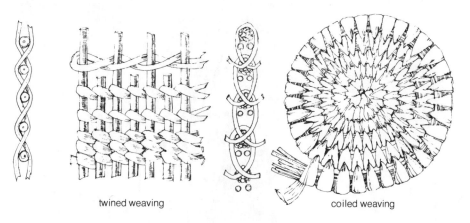

twined weaving   coiled weaving

Fig. 171. Two major types of weaving

■ The leftover inside core of splints is used for the foundation rods and the outside or sapwood used for the splints. Other materials such as flat bark strips and rush strips can also be used for splints.

Large burden sacks, packs, blankets, storage-pit liners, clothing, and sandals are made from the inner soft bark of the sagebrush and cliffrose plants. The strips of bark are fluffed and slightly twisted for the warp strands. Cords and flat strips are used for the weft. A loose twined weave is sufficient for the burden sacks and packs. Sandals are easily made from the bark in a few hours. Time does not usually permit refinement of the sandals, but serviceable ones can be twined in about three hours and will last through about three days of moderate use (Figs. 172–175).

Fig. 172. Blanket woven from bark

Fig. 173. Size of woven blanket

Fig. 174. Twined basket made from bulrush

Fig. 175. Sandals woven from bark

Woven water jugs are merely coiled baskets with small openings at the top. They are lined with pitch that is smeared on the inside before the constricting top is made. The remainder is then lined in this way: a lump of pitch is placed inside the basket with a hot rock and the container is shaken until the pitch has melted and has spread over the surface. One prepares pine pitch by boiling lumps of it for about 15 minutes and then skimming off the surface with a flat stick. It must then be heated when used. Another method consists of burning the pitch on a sloping rock. The turpentine burns away, and the pure pitch runs down the rock to where it can be collected and molded into small balls.

Baskets can be made watertight without the pitch liner if they are constructed with a very tight coiled weave. The advantage of this is that one can boil water in them by merely placing hot stones in the baskets, a process called stone boiling. Food can also be prepared by the same stone boiling process, but instead of a basket a skin or a paunch is used.

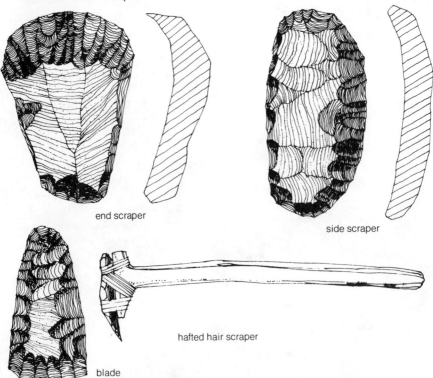

end scraper

side scraper

hafted hair scraper

blade

Fig. 176. Stone scrapers

Making Rawhide

Making good rawhide requires a little more care than just letting a green hide dry until it is stiff. Several steps must be taken to render it usable for moccasin soles, bags, pails, ropes, boxes, and other utilitarian items.

- ■ The hide must be soaked in water a day or more if it has previously been dried out, but if it is green this step is not necessary.
- ■ The hide is staked out with the flesh side up, and all of the fat and excess tissue is scraped off with a flesher, which is made from a long bone of a large animal. One side is honed down to a very sharp edge and small teeth are cut in it. Then a strap is fastened to the top to serve as a wrist support. The implement is used in a hacking manner to peel and scrape the fat from the hide. Stone scrapers are held in the hand and applied in a drawing motion across the hide (Fig. 177).

Fig. 177. Scraping off fat and excess tissue

Fig. 178. Hide staked for scraping

■ The hide is washed and cleaned and left staked out for a couple of days to dry in the sun. During the washing process the scrapers should be used to check that all fat is removed. Water is normally used for cleaning but better results can be achieved by using urine. This may be repulsive to most people, but it stands proven as a superior way of cleaning a hide. The urine should soak into the hide until the fat is completely dissolved by

Fig. 179. Frame stretching

the strong acids. It is then scraped off, along with the dissolved fat. The urine cleaning is followed with a good washing of water.

■ The hide, after it is dry and stiff and after the stakes are removed from it, is turned over and restaked. All of the hair is removed with a hair scraper. A sideways motion is used and every inch of the hide is covered. This back-breaking work is somewhat easier if the hide is soaked in a wood-ashes solution overnight. This loosens the hair and allows it to slip out rather than be shaved off by the hair scraper. Hair scrapers are simply small hoes made of wood, bone, or horn with a sharp stone blade attached to the hoe end. The blade must be sharpened often (Fig. 176—bottom).

■ The final step in making rawhide is to place the dry hide on a soft pad of grass or old blankets and to pound it with a blunt stone hammer weighing about three or four pounds. The hide should be struck with short glancing blows, and every inch of it must be covered if the grain is to be broken and if the hide is to become white and soft. Rawhide prepared this way is just as tough as tanned shoe leather and almost as soft.

Tanning Skins—Tools for Tanning

Tanning skins in the wilds requires special tools. Circumstances in a primitive setting often limit the availability of certain resources, so some of the tools listed here have alternates which, though often more difficult to use, will serve the purpose. Also, slightly different methods are adaptable to different locales and levels of lifestyle. Once mastered, they will produce the same results.

Stretching Tools

Skins must be stretched several times during the tanning process. There are two basic methods.

■ Frame stretching requires sturdy poles, lashings, and about one hundred feet of small-diameter rope or lacing. The frame poles are set up (Fig. 179) with lashings and braces so that the inside dimensions are approximately one foot larger than the hide to be tanned. The lacing rope may be simple baling twine, rawhide cord, yucca strips, or dried and twisted cattail leaves. A long cord will enable continuous lacing, while natural plant cordage involves short strips tied onto the frame separately.

■ Ground stretching makes the graining process in tanning more difficult and also requires the tanner to work in a stooped or kneeling position. However, the actual stretching process is much simpler and requires only a smooth ground surface and wooden stakes. The stakes are made from hardwood shoots about 3/4 inch indiameter and 12 to 14 inches long. Each stake should have a piece of cord wrapped tightly around its top end to prevent it from splitting while being pounded into the ground.

Scrapers

Fleshing tools can be made of steel, bone, or stone. Steel stays sharp longer but is no better than bone or stone for doing the job. Stone hand scrapers are easy to make but are more difficult to use because they tire the arms. (See also Working Stone, for details on flaking stone.)

The long bone scrapers with a wrist strap is better; it is relatively easy to make and sharpen (Fig. 180). Long leg bones of deer, elk, cow, horse, or other large animal are split and honed down by

Fig. 180. Bone fleshing tool

Fig. 181. Bone fleshing tool with toothed edge

rubbing on a sanding stone. The chisel-shaped cutting edge is then serrated to produce jagged griping tines. A strap is tied on the top end of the scraper and looped to form a wrist brace (Fig. 181).

Hafted stone or steel blades make excellent scrapers and may be made in a variety of shapes and sizes (Fig. 182 and 183). Hafting increases power and pressure for scraping hides. Tools for tanning should be made easy to disassemble for sharpening and blade replacement. This is accomplished by wrapping with buckskin, cordage, or string rather than sinew and pitch. Knots should also be easy to undo. Bone handles are especially suited to socket and wedge hafting when a stone blade is fitted in the socket and wedged there. Hoe-shaped scrapers should be large and heavy for best results.

Fig. 182. Hafted stone scraper

Hair Scrapers

Removing hair from hides requires a fine cutting edge, and steel or stone are the only scrapers that work well. Bone- or antler-handled hafted scrapers are good, and the hoe-shaped heavy ones are best. Be sure to make the blades with razor edges. Stone blades are best made using sharp blanks with edges that are not retouched (Fig. 176). (See also Working Stone, for details on blade-making.)

Graining Tools

There are two types of rubbing and graining tools. The first has a sharp or wedge-shaped blade which may be made of wood (Fig. 184). Some of the hide scrapers listed above will serve as blade graining tools.

The second type needed is a blunt, rounded edge on a heavy pole or stick (Fig. 185). This tool must be smooth and without any sharp edges. It is used with greater pressure in the graining process.

Fig. 183. Stone graining tool

Fig. 184. Hafted stone scraper

Fig. 185. Blunt wooden graining tool

Rubbing and Sanding Stones

Tanning stones are handheld and shaped like a flattened loaf. They should be smooth and free of irregular edges. They are used to rub on the brains in the tanning process.

Sanding stones may be any rough pieces of pumice or sandstone that will act like sandpaper in rubbing off hard-to-clean areas and in sanding off rough areas on the surface of the skin (Fig. 186).

Skinning and Care of Hides

Any animal skin can be made useful, tanned or untanned. At least one of my students kept enough pelts from his trapline to fashion some finger mittens of untanned mouse skins! (Fig. 187.)

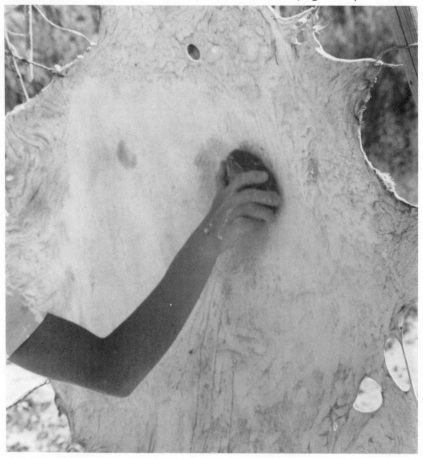

Fig. 186. Rubbing stone

Skinning

Depending on what you want to do with them, pelts may be cased or split. Casing a hide means pulling the entire skin off the carcass from the rear forward, with cuts made only around the feet of the animal and from the back legs to the tail. This method allows the skin to be made into mittens, bags, quivers, and other holding utensils. It is also the standard method of pelting many fur-bearing animals for the fur market.

Splitting a skin involves the same procedures as casing, but the hide is split up the legs and all the way up the belly to the chin and the hide is laid out flat.

Raw or Green Skins

At the very least, a hide may be dried and used as a stiff bag or laid out flat as bedding. Green hides are warm and can be formed into stiff, body-hugging quilts in an emergency.

On one occasion, with a group of survival trainees, I butchered a large buck sheep (which lasted only one meal) and we threw the hide over a limb. Later that evening, because of the "sardine"

Fig. 187. Mouse skin finger mitten

conditions, I relinquished my sleeping spot in our small cave. I pulled that green, wet hide off the tree and, with a little help from one of the guys, wrapped up tightly with the wool side in. My knees were tucked up, my feet just fit inside, and my head was covered. Neatly wrapped and tucked in, I spent the night just outside the cave. Toward morning it snowed, then cleared off, and the temperature dropped near zero. I needed help to get out of my solid cocoon, which was frozen stiff, but it was toasty warm inside.

Green hides can be dried for keeping by laying or hanging them out in the open air and sunlight. No parts should be allowed to overlap or be folded, as flies and moisture will spoil the skin quickly. Dried skins should be given a preliminary scraping to remove the major pieces of flesh and fat that might spoil and damage the skin. Thin layers of flesh will dry along with the hide and will not need removal until the tanning process is begun. Dried skins will keep a long time. However, salted hides do not brain tan as well.

Animal Hide Uses

A skin's uses in a primitive setting are limited only by the imagination. Listed below are a few ideas which have been tested in survival and primitive living camps:

- Deer, elk, moose, antelope, horse, calf, cow, goat, leather and rawhide with the hair removed: best used for clothing, footgear, straps, snowshoes, quivers, bags, string, rope, hinges, bowstrings, snare lines, sewing laces, boxes, pack sacks and frames, hafting wrap, and so forth. **Note:** Hollow-haired animals such as deer, elk, and antelope do not tan well with the hair left on, and they shed badly.
- Horse, cow, calf, sheep, mountain goat, bear, cougar, bobcat, wolf, marten, coyote, weasel, mink, beaver, otter, racoon, skunk, leather and rawhide with the hair left on: best used for robes, bedding, clothing, bags, quivers, hats, cold weather footgear, fur linings, and so on.
- Badger, wolverine, porcupine, leather and rawhide with hair left on or removed: moccasin soles, bags, quivers, chipping pads, hats, cold weather footgear, etc. Badger is noted as a tough hide for moccasin soles, but its value as a fur makes it uneconomical for this use except in emergencies.
- Rabbit, muskrat, rockchuck, packrats, mice, and other small rodents, leather and rawhide with hair left on: bags, string, hats,

mittens, fur liners for footgear, clothing, twisted-fur-strip blankets, and ponchos.

■ Birds skinned with feathers intact and dried, lightly tanned: sew inside clothing for extra warmth; breast skins sewn together for warm robe or poncho; feathers and down plucked from skins are useful as insulation, and may be twisted into warm feather cord blankets.

■ Snakes, lizards, and other reptiles, leather and rawhide: small pouches, wrappings for handles, small sealers and wraps for moisture protection, and so on.

The Tanning Process

With the tools in hand and information well in mind, tanning may be a swift process taking from six to ten actual working hours, the curing time spreading the whole process over two or three days. Skins vary in thickness. Each has its own qualities which must be dealt with in order to produce leather or soft furs. The process below uses a deerskin as the example. The steps are the same for all skins tanned with the hair removed. Furs and hides tanned with the hair on require a little more gentle handling and, of course, the step for hair removal is skipped.

■ Dry skins must be soaked in water until thoroughly soft. A fresh green hide need not be soaked if it is to be stretched right away. Soaking may be done by sinking the hide in a ditch or stream or tying it to the bank with a rope and letting it drag in fast running water. Some tanners will let a skin drag in cold swift water for a week, or until the hair has all been slipped and forced off by the water pressure. To do this, tie the anchor rope near the tail so that the current will run against the hair grain. The epidermis is more easily scraped off after the hair is gone. However, the time involved makes this step impractical in a survival situation.

Most skins can be softened overnight by soaking them in a container of cool water. If the skin is left in longer than twelve hours, check it often and change the water if it gets scummy. Upon removing it from the water, scrub the skin to help remove blood and debris.

Stretching

A fresh green or soaked hide must be stretched immediately and pulled tight with the flesh side up.

■ If the hide is stretched on a frame, begin with the head and lace the cord loosely around the frame and through small holes punched in the edges of the hide about three inches apart. As you progress around the hide and frame, begin pulling the lacing tight until the whole skin is taut. If using short pieces of cord, pull the cords tight from opposite sides and work back and forth until an even stretch is achieved. This takes about an hour (Fig. 188).

Fig. 188. Stretching on a frame

- Ground stretching is less difficult, but it makes scraping harder. Perfectly level ground is a must. The hide is spread out with the flesh side up and a stake is driven through a hole punched at the head. Then drive a stake at the tail, pulling the hide tight. Go back and forth at opposite ends, driving stakes about every three to five inches, and pulling the skin tight with each stake. The holes in the skin are punched with a large bone awl or knife before each stake is driven. Driving stakes is easier if a steel stake is used to punch a hole in the ground and is then removed and the wooden one pounded in. This saves wooden stakes from being beaten down or broken if they hit a rock (Fig. 189).

Fleshing

Whether you use steel, stone, or bone tools, the process is the same for fleshing a hide. Scrape and hack off all of the flesh, membrane, and fat adhering to the hide while it is wet. If only hand scrapers of stone are available, it may work better to let the hide dry, then scrape hard, pulling the membrane off in sheets. One benefit of dry scraping is that you salvage membrane sheets which may be cut in strips and used in the same way as sinew for hafting.

Scraping begins at the head and progresses down to the tail. Be careful not to make holes in the more tender parts of the belly,

Fig. 189. Stretching on ground

flank and tail area. Scrub and wash bloody areas as you scrape. Soapy water (nondetergent soapflakes) or yucca root helps this process if it is available. Restretch the hide if it loosens, and let it dry after scraping it.

Dehairing

Turn the dry skin over with the hair side up. Two things come off the hide in this process—the hair and the epidermis or first layer of skin. The hide will not remain soft if the epidermis is left on. The best scraper for dehairing is the hoe-shaped heavy one, with a steel or stone blade. Bone-bladed scrapers will not work. The prime factor is the sharpness of the blade. The blades will need sharpening frequently. Stone-bladed scrapers are best without retouched edges, which require switching blades every few minutes, but retouching will work if done carefully so that no jagged edges remain on the blade. (See Working Stone for details of retouching or pressure flaking stone blades.)

With careful, even strokes, beginning at the head, scrape off the hair and epidermis, working down the hide toward the tail. It will be impossible to get the hair off around the edges close to the lacings or stakes. This part is left alone and will be removed when the hide is cut from the frame or stakes.

Braining

The agent that breaks down the glue or glycerin and loosens the fibers of the skin is found in the brains of animals. Generally, a moose brain is sufficient in quantity to tan a moose hide, a mouse brain will tan a mouse skin, and so forth. However, any brain will do for any kind of skin if the quantity is sufficient. There are many receipes for preserving brains until the skin is ready for tanning. A few are as follows:

- Slightly cook the brains in a little water and completley mash and squeeze them between your fingers, pulling at the fibrous membranes until the mixture is too hot to keep your hands in. Then spread the thin oily mixture on a smooth board and lay it out to dry. It will keep several days in a cool place. When ready to use it, peel it off the board and reconstitute in water, slightly cooking it in the process.
- Mix the heated brains together with the moss found hanging from pine trees, form into small cakes, and dry. The moss acts

Fig. 190. Cooked brains

Fig. 191. Rubbing on the brain tanning solution

as a binder and can be removed from the mixture when it is reconstituted.

■ Cook the brains until yellow and mix with the spinal cord; put mixture in an intestine casing like sausage and seal the ends. This will keep in a cool place for several days. To reconstitute, cook in a little water until hot to the touch.

In every case, the delicate brain mix is cooked lightly, which increases its keeping quality. Raw brains, if left out, will spoil and smell bad in just a few hours. Fresh brains are preferred over any of the above and if obtained at the right time, or if kept frozen, will do a better job. Just cook, smash, and apply (Figs. 190 and 191).

There are other tanning agents which, though often easier, are not as good nor as obtainable in the wilderness setting. Used in a similar way as the brains, egg whites, real soap flakes (nondetergent), or even lard will effect a bacterial breakdown of the glue or glycerin material in the skin.

When the brains are prepared for tanning, there should be a soupy thick mixture surrounded by a thin broth in the container. Smear the thick paste mixture on the skin starting with the flesh side, then put what is left on the hair side (of a dehaired skin). Use your warm hands and heated tanning stones to rub the mixture in. Then, with a brush or rag, brush on the broth that's left in the brain container. This will thin the paste and cause the brains to soak in better. Let the mixture absorb into the skin for six hours or more before going on to the next step.

Graining

The skin should be quite damp and somewhat pliable with the brains on. Also, its thickness will have increased. Sponge on water to further dampen the skin; unstake or unlace and again soak the skin in water, submerging it overnight. Skins with the hair left on should not be soaked, but dampen them by applying warm water on the flesh side. Warm, wet rags speed up the process.

If soaking the skin in a container, it is nice to add some pounded yucca root or biscuit root to the water and suds it up. This helps clean the pores and removes the animal smell from the hide. Regular nondetergent soapflakes will also help if available.

The next day, remove the hide from the water. If the stretcher was used, restretch the skin on the frame and use the wedge-shaped graining tool to ooze the water from the hide. Apply pressure over every inch and scrape and stretch the fibers until most of the water is gone from the skin. Then, with the blunt graining pole, go over the entire hide again, stretching and rubbing until the skin is nearly dry but still slightly damp and cool to the touch. This may take an hour, though sunlight will speed up the drying process. The secret to tanning is in how well you keep the fibers in the hide stretched while it is drying!

Next, cut the skin from the frame around the perimeter, leaving only the lacing holes and hair that could not be removed before. If time won't permit the final step of rubbing, roll the skin up and store it in a plastic bag or slightly damp cloth.

If the hide has been staked to the ground during the earlier tanning process, then a little different procedure is needed, since the stretching frame is not available. After trimming off the rough edges of the skin, wring it out by twisting it on a stick.

Although more difficult, the same graining effect can be achieved by binding the blade graining tool to an upright post about 4½ feet from the ground and pulling the skin back and forth across it, covering every inch of both sides. Then do the same with the blunt graining pole. Repeat until the skin is cool and only slightly damp to the touch.

Rubbing

The next critical step of tanning is the high-friction rubbing needed to create a little heat and finish the drying, stretching, and breaking of the grain. A number of methods can be used, depending on what is available:

■ Use a ½ inch rope attached to a tree limb about seven feet from the ground. Attach the other end to the tree trunk, leaving a taut, upright cord. First stretch the hide by placing it smoothly around the rope loop and pulling it hard. The skin will stretch noticeably. Grasp the skin at different points all around its permieter and pull, pull, pull. When the skin is stretched, begin the friction process by pulling the hide back and forth in a see-saw motion over the rope. Rub it all around the perimeter and from every angle until the entire hide is completely dry. The final product will be white and soft.

■ If a rope is not available, stretch the skin by sitting on the ground and hooking the skin over your feet and pulling. Then hook the skin around a slender, smooth sapling and generate the friction. A better rubbing method is to make a pole blade by

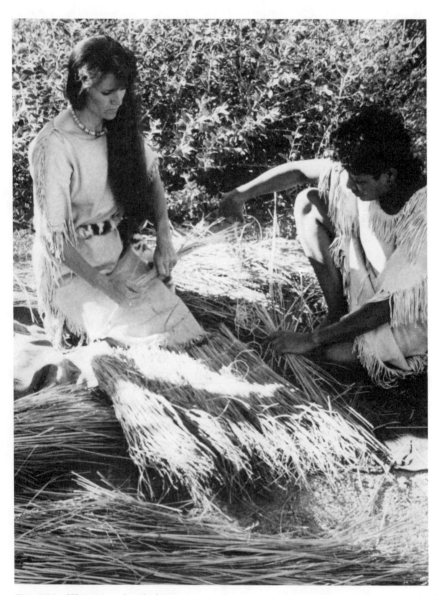

Fig. 192. Women in buckskins

beveling one edge and securing it between two posts. Pull the skin back and forth over it to stretch and dry it.

When the skin is completely dry, it may be finished with sanding stones. Any area of the skin that is blemished, rough, or spotted can be sanded to produce a fluffy texture overall. Use the stones like sandpaper.

The tanning is essentially finished at this point. The leather is white and ready to use for clothing and general purposes.

Smoking

When a white tanned skin gets wet, it will often dry stiff and need reworking to restore the softness. Smoking the hide will help prevent this and also give the skin a buckskin brown color and pleasant woodsmoke aroma.

Sew up the skin into a large bag or tube with the tail and head ends left open. Attach the head end to a crosspole and stake the base down over a small but deep firepit which should be from six to ten inches deep and filled with glowing hot coals. Leave a small opening at the base of the tube where you can drop some punk or wet or green wood chips on the hot coals. Sage or willow are good woods, although any type, will work. The object is to get the chips to smoke, not burn. Careful watching, and a handful of dirt kept ready, are necessary to prevent flames from ruining the hide. It only takes a few minutes to brown the skin, and the longer it is left, the deeper becomes the color. Smoke one or both sides, as desired. After smoking, roll up the hide and put it away in a bag for a day. This lets the smoke sink in and become a permanent part of the skin. The aroma of smoked leather will remain as long as the leather lasts.

APPENDIX

The following colorplates identify numerous plants used to fulfill a variety of outdoor needs.

The pictures are arranged alphabetically by common name. Appearing below the common name(s) are the scientific— generic and species—names (in italics). The different uses of the plant—as food, medicine, tinder, fiber—are listed last.

The pictures of edible plants are of specific genera and species. Therefore, in many cases they are only representative (being among the most common species growing in the western United States) of particular genera appearing in the list of edible plants in Chapter 5 (pp. 52–89).

Some plants which are edible are also poisonous unless prepared with caution; others are easily confused with poisonous plants. Therefore, to aid the reader and to caution him, a † precedes each of these.

Amaranth
Amaranthus retroflexus
Food

Arrowhead
Sagittaria latifolia
Food

Arrowleaf Balsamroot
Balsamorrhiza sagittata
Food

Colorplate 1

Asparagus
Asparagus officinalis
Food

Beeplant
Cleome lutea
Food

Beeplant
Cleome serrulata
Food

Colorplate 2

†Biscuit-root
Cymopterus bulbosus
Food, Medicine

Blazing Star
Mentzelia laevicaulis
Food

Bluegrass
Poa longiligula
Food

Colorplate 3

†Bracken Fern
Pteridium aquilinum
Food

†Bracken Fern
Pteridium aquilinum
Food

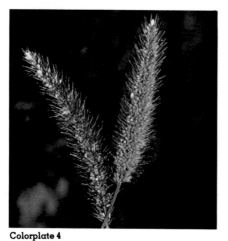

Bristlegrass
Setaria viridis
Food

Colorplate 4

188

Bulrush
Scirpus
Food, Fiber

Bulrush
Scirpus acutus
Food, Fiber

Burdock
Arctium minus
Food, Medicine

Colorplate 5

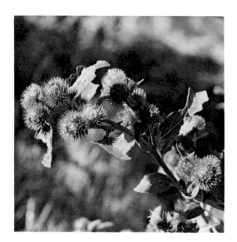

Burdock
Arctium minus
Food, Medicine

Burreed
Sparganium euricarpum
Food

†Camas
Camassia quamash
Food

Colorplate 6

190

†Camas
Camassia quamash
Food

†Camas—Death Camas
Zigadenus paniculatus
Poisonous

Colorplate 7

Cattail
Typha latifolia
Food, Medicine, Tinder,
Fiber, Tools

†Chokecherry
Prunus virginiana
Food, Medicine, Tools

Cliffrose
Cowania mexicana
Tinder, Fiber

Cottonwood
Populus deltoides
Food, Tinder

Colorplate 8
192

Currant
Ribes
Food, Tools

Dogbane
Apocynum cannabinum
Tinder, Fiber

†Elderberry
Sambucus caerulea
Food

Colorplate 9

Evening Primrose
Oenothera hookeri
Food

Goldenrod
Solidago
Food

Colorplate 10

Greasewood
Sarcobatus
Food—Tools

Ground Cherry
Physalis fendleria
Food

Groundsel
Senecio
Food

Hairgrass
Deschampsia elongata
Food

Colorplate 11

195

Heron's Bill
Erodium cicutarium
Food

Heron's Bill
Erodium cicutarium
Food

Horsetail
Equisetum hyemale
Food

Colorplate 12

Indian Potato
Orogenia linariifolia
Food

Indian Potato
Orgenia linariifolia
Food

Indian Ricegrass
Oryzopsis hymenoides
Food

Colorplate 13

Jerusalem Artichoke
Helianthus tuberosus
Food

Jerusalem Artichoke
Helianthus tuberosus
Food

Juniper
Juniperus osteosperma
Food

Colorplate 14

Juniper
Juniperus osteosperma
Food, Tinder, Fiber

Lamb's Quarter
Chenopodium album
Food

Mallow
Malva neglecta
Food

Colorplate 15

199

Maple
Acer negundo
Food

†Milkweed
Asclepias speciosa
Food, Fiber

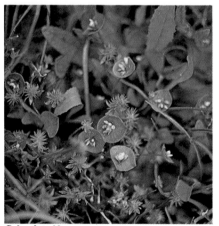

Miner's Lettuce
Montia perfoliata
Food

Colorplate 16

200

Mint
Mentha
Food

Mint
Mentha
Food

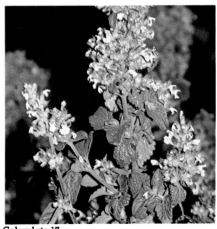

Mint
Nepeta cataria
Food

Colorplate 17

201

Mormon Tea
Ephedra
Food

Mountain Dandelion
Agoseris aurantiaca
Food

Mule's Ears
Wyethia amplexicaulis
Food

Colorplate 18

202

Mullein
Verbascum thapsus
Medicine, Tinder

Mustard
Brassica nigra
Food

Mustard
Cardaria draba
Food

Colorplate 19

Mustard
Lepidium perfoliatum
Food

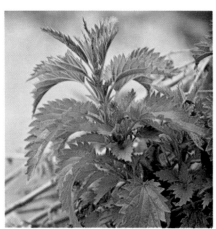

Nettle
Urtica gracilis
Food, Medicine, Tinder, Fiber

†Oak
Quercus gambelii
Food

Colorplate 20

204

†Onion
Allium acuminatum
Food, Medicine

†Onion
Allium textile
Food, Medicine

Colorplate 21

Oregon Grape
Mahonia aquifolium
Food

205

Oregon Grape
Mahonia fremontii
Food

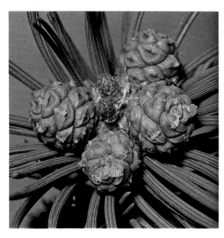

Piñon Pine
Pinus edulis
Food

Plantain
Plantago lanceolata
Food, Medicine

Colorplate 22

Prickly Lettuce
Lactuca scariola
Food

Prickly Lettuce
Lactuca scariola
Food

Prickly Pear Cactus
Opuntia phaeacantha
Food

Colorplate 23

Prickly Pear Cactus
Opuntia polyacantha
Food

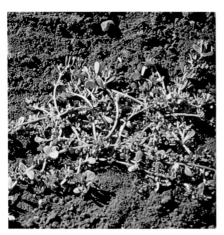

Purslane
Portulaca oleracea
Food

†Rabbitbrush
Chrysothamnus nauseosus
Food

Colorplate 24

Raspberry
Rubus idaeus
Food

Red Clover
Trifolium pratense
Food

Reed
Phragmites communis
Food, Tinder, Fiber, Tools

Colorplate 25

Rose
Rosa
Food, Medicine, Tools

Sagebrush
Artemisia tridentata
Tinder, Fiber

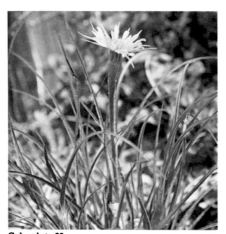

Salsify
Tragopogon dubius
Food

Colorplate 26

Salsify
Tragopogon dubius (yellow)
Tragopogon porrifolius (purple)
Food

Samphire
Salicornia pacifica
Food

Sego Lily
Calochortus nuttallii
Food

Colorplate 27

Serviceberry
Amelanchier alnifolia
Food, Medicine, Tools

†Sorrel Dock
Rumex hymenosepalus
Food, Medicine

†Sour Dock
Rumex crispus
Food, Medicine

Colorplate 28

212

Spring Beauty
Claytonia lanceolata
Food

Strawberry
Fragaria vesca
Food

Sumac
Rhus trilobata
Food

Sunflower
Helianthus annuus
Food, Tinder

Thistle
Cirsium undulatum
Food, Tinder

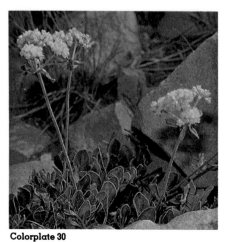

Umbrella Plant
Eriogonum alpinum
Food

Colorplate 30

214

Violet
Erythronium grandiflorum
Food

Watercress
Rorippa nasturium-aquaticum
Food

Waterleaf
Hydrophyllum capitatum
Food

Colorplate 31

215

†Wild Hyacinth
Brodiaea douglasii
Food

Yarrow
Achillea millefolium
Medicine

Yellow Fritillary
Fritillaria pudica
Food

Colorplate 32

INDEX

217